Money Is No Object

How to Get the Life You Dream of,
Even if You Think You Can't Afford it.

A Guide for Resourceful Women

Money Is No Object

How to Get the Life You Dream of,
Even if You Think You Can't Afford it.

A Guide for Resourceful Women

Deborah G. Hining,
PhD, CFP®, ChFC, CLU, CRPC
CERTIFIED FINANCIAL PLANNER®

⟩Light Messages

Copyright© 2011 Deborah Griffitts Hining

Money is no Object: How to Get the Life You Dream of,
  Even if You Think You Can't Afford it.
  A Guide for Resourceful Women
Deborah Griffitts Hining

Published 2011, by Light Messages
www.lightmessages.com
Durham, NC 27713 USA
SAN: 920-9298

ISBN: 978-0-9800756-8-7

Author's Note

As a woman in a male dominated profession, it was clear to me from the beginning that testosterone is a mighty force, and that if I didn't want to become overwhelmed by it, I would either have to start manufacturing my own or find some antidote in order to survive.

The research behind *Money is No Object* provided that antidote. My investigation, both scholarly and empirical, of gender-based differences of values, thoughts, and resources, has led me to appreciate the many assets women possess. In every society, in every age, women have always found ways to make things better. As we learn to fully use our feminine gifts to the best advantage, even in a male-dominated world or profession, we can create a better life for ourselves, our families, and the people we serve.

Of course, this book has taken more time, effort, energy, and people to bring together than I ever dreamed that it could. Without the help, encouragement, and love of many around me, it would never have made it this far. I especially want to thank those on my stellar staff who put up with my obsession and helped me in innumerable ways: Chris, Julie, and Lewis, you were a godsend; and Alyce, Angela, and Daniel, you also inspired me with your gifts and talents. You all kept me sane and encouraged with your good humor and grace.

Also thanks to those clients and friends who were willing to slog through very bad early drafts and offer suggestions for improvement. A special thanks to the lovely Anne, who gave me honest and insightful criticism far beyond what I expected. Tom, Carla, Susan, Sarah, Britt, Pabby, Betty, Wally, Lisa, Mike, and Mary Elizabeth, the fact that you were willing to read and offer suggestions gave me hope and kept me from giving up. Marcia, I am indebted to you and your stellar proofreading abilities. Janet, your wisdom, good humor, and guidance kept me from the abyss of absolute failure during my first three years in this business. Thank you for being such a kind and sensitive boss.

And finally, thanks to Sean Rowe, in memoriam: a friend and an encourager who believed in this project.

To my father, my husband, my son, and my son-in-law,
four strong men who have always appreciated
the strengths of women.

TABLE OF CONTENTS

MONEY IS NO OBJECT

If you picked up this book thinking it will help you make a budget or get your finances in order, be warned—or be heartened. It isn't so dull as that, although it will help you improve your financial (and personal) well-being by helping you to understand how to better utilize all your assets more fully. It is half history lesson, half philosophy, and half financial wizardry (See, it's working already. Only magic could make that add up).

As a financial planner who has been helping people for over 17 years to dream bigger, live their passions, and become who they want to be by taking personal risk (within reason), I have learned that our real resources lie within ourselves. How much money we have in an investment portfolio is insignificant compared to the simple gifts of dreams, talents, and ambitions. These are the things that open up a life of riches for ourselves and for those we love.

Thank you for reading this book. I hope it launches you on a big, scary, exhilarating journey that takes you places you only hoped you could dream of. At the very least, I hope it helps you understand how fabulously wealthy you are.

FOREWORD

I am very definitely a woman, and I enjoy it
~Marilyn Monroe

When my mother was eight years old, she ran a thriving bootlegging enterprise. During those prohibition years, good whiskey was hard to come by, so her father, somewhat less ambitious but with a miscreant thirst, employed a local moonshiner to produce corn liquor he knew would be safe enough for his own consumption. When his father-in-law discovered the existence of the clandestine operation, he recruited my mother to skim a little off the jug each day and make regular refreshment runs to his house. He paid well, according to my mother: well enough, in fact, for her to be able to keep herself, her mother, and her siblings fed during the lean times when my grandfather was too drunk from his own recipe to provide for the family.

A few years later, during the Great Depression, she and her sisters and brothers continued to help support the family by keeping a garden plot, picking wild berries, and fishing in the river. They kept chickens and cows and butchered a hog every fall. They ate well during the summer months, and they were able to can and dry enough food to see them through the winters. They often sold some of the excess. New Easter shoes came from money they saved from peddling blackberries, huckleberries, and muscadine grapes all over the county. And, of course, moonshine on occasion, when Pap-pa was thirsty.

My mother did not consider her activities unusual. Bartering, farming, and gathering the resources of the wild were more the rule for economic activity than the monetary standard by which we operate today. Schoolteachers,

Deborah Griffitts Hining

preachers, doctors, and even storekeepers were paid, not from hard cash, but from the fruits of the earth and the goods people were able to manufacture at home from them. People traded a herd of cattle for land in Texas; a lump of gold found in a North Carolina stream served as payment for a fine horse and carriage. A length of wool woven from sheep in Montana might have been traded for the services of a blacksmith.

No doubt you have heard stories in your own family about how an itinerant doctor was paid a cured ham or a bushel of ground corn for a difficult birthing or for saving the life of a snakebite victim or how your great-great aunt boarded with the families of the children she taught in her tiny frontier school. Housewives for millenniums have traded their extra butter and eggs for scraps of ribbon or a packet of sewing needles.

The very idea of paying someone wages or paying cash for goods or services rendered is a pretty new concept in human history. Money has been around for only about 2,650 years, and it is much more recent that we, the general populace, have begun to think it as about the only means to procure the stuff necessary to maintain life. As a separate entity, used strictly as a standardized unit of exchange, money wasn't invented until around 635 BC.

Although the ancients used it fairly regularly, coinage was not the only currency used in those times. Soldiers in the Ancient Roman Empire were often paid in salt. The very word "salary" is derived from the root of "salt." The expression we use today that someone is "worth his salt" comes from the literal meaning.[1]

As the Roman Empire began to fail (thanks largely to overconsumption, greed, corruption, and endless warring), the government debased the coinage so severely by mixing base metals in with the precious that money became worthless. With the final collapse of the Empire and the onset of the Dark Ages, coinage more or less disappeared as the primary means of buying and selling.

During the next few centuries, land and foodstuff were considered about the only things of value. People abandoned the decaying cities and moved to large estates, where they worked as serfs. Their labors were rewarded, not with cash, but with a portion of the crops they grew on the landholders' estates. Servants were rarely paid anything at all up until the 14th century in Europe. It was enough to receive the shelter and protection of the lord's castle keep and to be fed on a regular basis.[2]

Many commodities and decorative items, ranging from almonds (India) to nubile young redheads from Ireland (Vikings) to Cowrie shells (the Maldives) have been used for money. Cattle have been considered a unit of money for many civilizations, and their importance in Europe has even shaped the language. The word "pecuniary," meaning "related to money" comes from the Latin "pecuniarius," meaning "wealthy in cattle."[3] "Impecunious," of course, means "poor," which I hope you are not, nor ever will be.

My favorite commodity used as currency was also favored by the ancient Aztecs, who otherwise were not the most sensible people in the world, being as how one of their favorite religious rituals was ripping out and eating the hearts of human sacrificial victims. After disemboweling corpses and hacking out and cooking the choicest body parts, the host of the big event would take them to the marketplace and sell them for—guess what? Chocolate! Actually, it was cacao beans, the primary monetary unit in the culture at that time,[4] but I like to imagine people walking around in the tropical climate, their pockets gooey with Godiva truffles. Why anyone would spend a perfectly

Deborah Griffitts Hining

wonderful hazelnut crème for a human liver or tongue is beyond me. Go figure.

Money was scarce to the common people until as late as the 18th century, and most local economies were largely based on the bartering of goods and services. Kings and the gentry had long used coinage, but for every member of the gentry or nobility found in Europe, Africa, or Asia, there were thousands of merchants, farmers, servants, slaves, serfs, tribesmen and women, and nomads. The welling masses who more fully populated the world and which make up the vast canopies of our family trees, saw money only in tiny quantities. And while you most likely have at least a drop of noble blood in your veins, and some of your way-back grandmothers had more than a farthing or two to rub together, statistically speaking, more of your ancestral line is made up of humbler folk who never saw the glimmer of gold.

No doubt you have a great-great-great grandmother who landed, filthy and sick, at the wharves in San Francisco to toil in the mining camps, or one served as an ignorant scullery maid in a great European household, or arrived by slave ship to work the plantations of Haiti. These are the grandmothers we celebrate here, each one who rarely saw more than a few pennies or a few dollars during her entire life. What little money she did see most likely was owned by her father or her husband or her master. She embraced poverty as a matter of course. To her there was no other state than simply living day to day, hand to mouth, and the things that would seem mere trifles to us—a bar of scented soap, a beeswax candle, a brooch—she would have considered the most fabulous and extravagant of luxuries.

And yet, she thrived. Your being here is a testimony to that. Most likely she knew happiness. She treasured friendship, knew what love felt like, had the pleasure of nursing babies. She laughed, sang, and prayed, and taught her children how to live rich, honest lives, and how to find fulfillment in the most fundamental activities of work and life.

She believed she had a storehouse full of resources, although she probably did not consider money one of them. She relied on her intelligence, her willing hands, her creativity, and her dreams to feather her own little nest. From her you have inherited thousands of things that have never occurred to you were from her, for deep in the recesses of your DNA, you hold the secret of how to live resourcefully, how to make much from little, and how to make the world better for yourself and those you love.

This book is dedicated to those women in our ancestral lines who had the wherewithal to make life a little richer with their physical, spiritual, and mental gifts. And to you, too, because you also can make it happen, with all the resources you have: the ones you know you have, and the ones you need to be reminded of.

CHAPTER 1

THE HERSTORY OF MONEY

If women didn't exist, all the money
in the world would have no meaning.
~Aristotle Onassis

In the Beginning was the Deed

What do we live for, if it is not to make
life less difficult for each other?
~George Eliot (MaryAnn Evans)

Let's start at the very beginning. In primitive societies, there was nothing like what we would call "money" today—small, easily exchanged tokens that represent certain values and can be used to buy and sell anything as concrete as today's lunch or as abstract as an hour on the therapist's couch. Before money came into being, people bartered or traded for goods ("I'll trade you my banana for your corn."). While bartering was useful, it tended to take place in an immediate context, for goods that could be used right away.

The first real currency that could be held and "banked" to be used over longer periods of time was a kind of social currency: favors given and received. Social currencies built stronger ties between people and were remembered informally. One person may "owe" another for a favor for weeks or months or longer, and the more the "currency" was traded back and forth, the stronger the social ties were built.[1]

Women have always excelled at using social currency, not only because we have been culturally conditioned to do so, but also because our brains are likely to be hardwired for nurturing and for forming emotional bonds. We'll delve into this more in subsequent chapters, but to make a generalized metaphor, we are born with large purses just stuffed with social currency, and we are constantly printing up more.

Women can get a lot done because of the social currency we pass back and forth among our friends and loved ones, and we enrich our lives and our friends' lives because we are willing to use this kind of exchange generously and without a lot of expectations.

You don't mind babysitting for your friend so she can go out on Saturday night, and you might feel free to call her when your battery dies and you need a ride to work. You will bake her a loaf of your homemade bread as a thank you for the ride, and then she will teach you how to crochet, without even considering that what you are doing for each other is actually worth money. Our spontaneous, emotional generosity causes us to want to do things for our friends, and that gives social currency its greatest value. We make our lives and each other's lives easier with this informal bartering of services.

Girl Power

Nobody gives you power. You just take it
~Roseanne Barr

Favors given and received, commodities that can be immediately consumed, labor, all these and many more things have been used as units of exchange since the beginning of human interaction. Money, or what we more or less know as "cash" today, was invented in the Greek state of Lydia in about 635 BC.

> You may have heard the expression "rich as Croesus," but did you know Croesus was the king of Lydia, who ascended the throne around 560 BC, about 75 years after money was birthed? Croesus, and Lydia, became fabulously, and famously, rich as a result of the commerce which grew up with the use of money.[2]

At first, money was democratic and genderless because it had not yet become linked with power, or even with the notion of "wealth." In those days, "wealth" meant titles, tangible commodities, and real estate—land, livestock, castles, luxuries—and one of its most important usages was to acquire and maintain power. Lydian women very quickly learned that they could turn money (the lowly coin) into power and independence.

In early Greek society, as it was during most of the vast scope of world history, women were not considered autonomous people. As children, and as female, they were the legal property of their fathers, and their value was measured by their ability to work (lower classes) or their ability to marry into other powerful families, and thereby increase the power and wealth of their fathers (upper classes). Especially important to a woman's value was her ability to bear children to work in the fields or ensure a continuation of an important family.

One of the primary duties of a father was to find suitable marriage partners for his children that would strengthen the family in some way. Suitability had nothing to do with how much a girl liked a potential mate. Marriage was strictly a financial and political merger, and was considered a *fait accompli* only after money exchanged hands.[3] A bride's father paid a dowry, and the family of the

Deborah Griffitts Hining

new husband paid or guaranteed by written contract a bride price (later called a "jointure").[4] Once married, the woman and whatever she owned became the property of her new husband.[5] That was just the way it was, and there was no getting around it, because by law and tradition, men controlled all the wealth and the power.

When money was newly invented, it was not considered "wealth," but just a unit of exchange that represented the ability to buy tangible, day-to-day goods. It was meant to be a convenient way to buy groceries for tonight's supper at the marketplace. But Lydian women immediately realized that they could sell goods and make money, and that would translate to the ability to acquire wealth. From there, they could accumulate their own dowries. And if they could provide their own dowries, they could be independent from their fathers. Economic independence meant they could claim the astonishing privilege of choosing their own husbands.

But what could they sell? That was trickier. They began to gather raw resources and manufacture things such as cosmetics and beauty products, and that proved to be very lucrative. Not only that, but they discovered a secret about men: they would pay good money for sex (something women had already figured out how to get for free millennia before), and they took full advantage of that fact. The first known brothels were built in a Lydian city, Sardis.[6] No doubt the status quo of Lydian society was less disturbed by the prostitution than the sudden financial autonomy of the girls who worked in the brothels.

This forward-thinking practice of women being economically independent and free to choose their own husbands died when the Lydian empire collapsed in 546 BC, and was not commonly accepted again for another 2,300 years.

The empire fell, by the way, because the citizens and the government became obsessed with materialism. I bring this up because I have a lot to say about it later. Ostentatious displays of wealth became a private and public pastime. When it became evident that merely manufacturing and selling goods would not fund the outrageously expensive projects everyone wanted, they happened on the bright idea of simply invading other countries and plundering their wealth. This worked for a while, until Croesus made the mistake of taking on the Spartans, who crushed Lydia and filled up their own coffers with everything the Lydians had acquired.

Housewives Rule!

Women can do everything;
men can do the rest.

~Russian proverb

Let's fast forward to some hundred years or so later. By this time, money had become more standardized, but it was still not considered the basis for wealth, which continued to be measured more commonly in property, livestock, slaves, commodities, and power. As a mere unit of exchange, it naturally was tied to the chore of running the household because it facilitated keeping account of the food stores and the household items necessary to keep a family clothed and fed. The economics of the home, and the idea of budgeting and planning for future needs fit logically into the realm of "women's work." Early on, women proved they had a good head about resource and money management.

The first book on economics was written by Xenophon of Athens in about 300 BC. Xenophon introduced the word *oikonomikos* (economics), which meant "skilled in managing a household or estate," and it was considered to be specifically a part of a woman's realm. The book, filled with practical domestic advice on how to manage a home, train servants, and preserve and store wine and food, compared women with the queen bee of the hive and assumed her to be responsible for all aspects of domestic life, including managing the money. The men were thus free to do more important things like wage war. When he wasn't writing books telling women how to do what they were already good at, Xenophon was a professional soldier.[7]

> Apparently, nobody had learned from Croesus' errors. War was still waged primarily to increase the wealth of a nation. Men saw it their responsibility to plunder to acquire lands, slaves and treasure, while the women were back home managing the nickels and dimes, and the day-to-day necessities of living. [8]

Oh, Goddess Divine!

When it is a question of money,
everybody is of the same religion

~Voltaire

The Romans also understood that money—still distinct from real wealth—should be held in the protective hands of women, and they expanded that notion to a larger scale. Juno, the highest Roman goddess, was patroness of the Roman state. As such, Juno was responsible for overseeing one of the primary activities of the state, issuing currency. In fact, Juno herself was responsible for the name we use for it today. In the fourth century BC, a tribe of Gauls, while attempting an assault on the citadel at Rome, disturbed the geese around Juno's temple so much they began honking in alarm. The invaders were thus discovered when they were halfway up the walls, and defenders were able to beat them back. From that time, Juno also became known as Juno Moneta, from the Latin monere (to warn). Her name, Moneta, is the root for the English word "money."[9]

Eventually, money became more of a symbol of true wealth, and men therefore began to take more notice in the general management of it. By the time the Roman Empire reached its height around 250 BC, men had fully become the minders of the mint in every way, at least in the upper circles of societies. The women were no longer in charge of the purses. I don't know if it was coincidence, but Rome went to hell in a handbasket after that, due primarily to the abuse and debasement of Rome's wealth. Again, conspicuous consumption and aggressive warmongering lead the country down the highway to total ruin.[10]

Helpmeets

If mama ain't happy, ain't nobody happy
~Unknown.
For years, I thought my daddy made it up.

After the fall of the Roman Empire in the late 5th century, the picture began to change. Money had become so abused and debased by the government and the moneyed classes that it eventually lost value altogether. Land, labor, and commodities became the primary unit of exchange, and once again, as in more primitive societies, women's work was considered just as valuable as men's.

Deborah Griffitts Hining

Peasants, pretty low on the social ladder, actually were not always the poverty stricken near-servants that we tend to think they were. Many peasants were actually considered "wealthy" by feudal standards. Most were farmers, but many were tradesmen and skilled craftsmen, and in most cases, the work of women was necessary to contribute to a family's well-being. Husbands and wives worked together as an economic unit to produce goods, and that meant partnership.

As contributing partners, women wielded considerable power within the family unit, despite their lowly status in society.[11] A husband technically owned his wife, and everything else belonging to the family, and he could beat her if she misbehaved, but anecdotal evidence suggests that women were quite often considered the "smart" ones of the family when it came to resource management. Also, men probably learned pretty early on that marital harmony was beneficial to their own well being when so much depended on family cooperation, so there may have been more leeway granted to wives than the laws of the time would indicate.

Queen Mothers

The Queene is queint, and quicke conceit,
Which makes her walke which way she list,. . .
Hir force is such against her foes,
That whom she meets, she overthrowes.
~from *The Chesse Play,*
by Nicholas Breton *(1542-1626)*

Because land, titles, and family ties were the most important economic and political considerations among the upper classes during medieval times, a woman of genteel birth also enjoyed a kind of status and economic power that both her forebears and descendants were not granted. At this time, the law of many lands supported the rule of queens, whereas later law limited that privilege. The general feeling among society at that time was that women actually were capable of handling power.

They did, however, tend to wield it differently than men. Although women were still usually merely the pawns of their families, they found some power in their connections and their ability to produce heirs and then counsel them. Many smart women found their own way of maneuvering.

Around 481, AD, Clothild, the orphaned niece of the king of Burgundy, thwarted her uncle's plan for her to marry one of his relatives so he could keep her dowry under his control. Secretly, she arranged a marriage with the Germanic king Clovis, and became his queen. She then convinced her husband to convert to Christianity, thus gaining an ally in the pope, and the official support and protection of the Roman Catholic Church.[12] Clothild became enormously powerful as a result of this. Not too shabby for a poor, ignorant orphaned girl!

The mothers of male heirs could work the system pretty well. Once sons gained power, their dear mamas came along for the ride. Because so much could be at stake, some women were not squeamish about conveniently getting the sons of their husbands' prior marriages out of the way via "accidents" or sudden "illnesses." Superfluous wives, mistresses, and pesky kinsmen also sometimes met some pretty horrific fates. Women seeking power (and to protect their children) plotted, schemed, made alliances, whispered "suggestions" to their husbands and lovers in bed, and built close friendships with important people, particularly church officials. They gave money, or cajoled their husbands and fathers into giving money to build monasteries and to fund nunneries. By buying the favor of the church, they gained power and used it to garner more power—and wealth.[13]

During the Middle Ages, so many women were instrumental in worldwide intrigue and politics that they inspired a name change in the most important and powerful piece in chess. This game, developed in India, initially had a queen piece, but she was ineffectual and weak. The powerful piece we call the Queen today was originally called the "Vizier," or consul to the King, named after the counselor who had the ear of the monarch.[14]

By changing the name of that piece to "Queen," medieval Europeans paid homage to the strength of the gentle ladies of the time. Powerful queens and noblewomen were common throughout Europe, and they proved themselves equal to men, even in an age when on the surface, women lacked basic freedoms. Margaret of Denmark united Denmark, Norway, and Sweden for the first time in history. Matilda of Tuscany led her troops to aid Pope Gregory VII. Queen Isabella of Spain ruled alongside her husband King Ferdinand and lobbied for Columbus' explorations.

Lower class women made their mark during this period as well. Joan of Arc, a French peasant girl led the French army to several important victories during the Hundred Years' War before she turned eighteen, and she was indirectly responsible for ascension of Charles VII to the throne. Of course, Joan of Arc was poor as dirt, but if she had not been burned at the stake and had had a good publicist, no doubt she would have been rolling in *francs*.

Wives

Who marrieth for love without money
hath good nights and sorry days.
~English Proverb (1670)

Still, while women were sometimes trusted with the economies of the household, and many finagled their way to personal power and wealth, in general, the lot of women was pretty dismal for most of history until feminism's giant leap forward in the middle of the 19th century. With few exceptions, women who did not marry were not recognized by law at all in most of the world from the beginning of civilization until modern times. An unmarried woman was entirely dependent upon her father, who had the right to beat, imprison, or even kill her for a number of astonishing reasons. Once married, both a woman and all her property belonged entirely to her husband. In England, the law in 1632 stated: "That which the husband hath is his own . . . That which the wife hath is the husband's."[15] That's a good bit different from a tee shirt I saw the other day worn by a young woman that read, "What's mine is mine. And what's his is mine too." Things sure have gotten better for the fair sex.

Male children also were considered the property of their fathers until they came of age and either joined the military or the church, or officially became the head of the household by taking a wife. Consequently, for the most part, a wedding was pretty much *the* watershed event in the lives of young people. As soon as a child was born, parents began saving for the day of the nuptials, much like parents today begin saving for college tuition, because a marriage could make or break the fortunes of both their child and themselves. It built or solidified very important political alliances,

Deborah Griffitts Hining

family connections, and claims to land and titles, which in turn, were linked to power and money.

And if you are wondering where love fit into betrothals and weddings, it didn't. Until the late 17th century, it was considered laughable that two people would consider that love, or even affection, should be the primary basis of marriage.[16] Although men made a show of "wooing" women they intended to marry with some romantic gestures, that show rarely lasted past the honeymoon.

Shakespeare was treading on new ground when he wrote *Romeo and Juliet* in 1595, which gave sympathetic treatment to young people who marry for love. Most of Shakespeare's audience would have identified with the consternation of the parents, when Lady Capulet throws a hissy fit over Juliet's refusal to marry the man her father has picked out for her. "I would the fool be married to her grave," she says, when Juliet digs in her heels.

Those harsh words were not considered appalling by late 16th century audiences. To give you a perspective, how would you react to your 13-year-old who declares she is dropping out of school to go live with the boy she met last night at a rock concert? That was exactly what Juliet was trying to pull. I think Lady Capulet probably reacted about like many a modern mom, who would be likely to speak in the contemporary vernacular: "You do, and I'll kill you."

Making a good marriage then was the equivalent of launching a great career today, and was the basis of economic stability of both individuals and the larger community.[17] And any deviation from that constituted a threat against society as a whole. Imagine if you were to refuse to take a fantastic job with excellent pay and benefits because you were not "in love" with your boss, meaning crazy about him in a romantic, sexual way. People would shake their heads and worry that society had run amok. Seriously, marriage was a business arrangement, with procreation being a very important element. That luvvy stuff like giggling together in bed, reading poetry, gazing longingly into each other's eyes—well, that was acceptable as long as it took place discretely between men and their mistresses (both of whom, incidentally, might be married to other people), but was considered tacky if it went on between husbands and wives. Marriage was too important to be cheapened by silly *amore*.[18]

Widows

What is earned in bed is collected in widowhood
~Early English folk saying

Girls tended to marry early, and since they regularly died young in childbirth, men often took several wives in succession. Men needed heirs, so they looked to marry girls with plenty of childbearing years before them. This meant that there frequently was a mismatch in ages between husbands and wives, and consequently, more than a bit of distaste on the part of the girl wed to someone past his prime.

But there was a positive side to these May-December weddings, and many canny women saw the advantage of it. Once widowed, European and English women did enjoy some economic advantages if they did not remarry, for they had personal access to the jointures provided by their husbands in the marriage contract. If they did remarry, widows were able to negotiate advantageous prenups because they had a measure of control.

Unlike wives and never married women, widows' rights were recognized by law, so they had far greater autonomy if and when they reached the exalted status of

Deborah Griffitts Hining

"widow" or "dowager."[19] During some periods, they even had the right to vote.

You might be interested to know that women from wealthy families who were widowed early and who never remarried tended to live to old age, enjoying a life of respect, ease, and considerable control over their families and the families' wealth. One young lady, about to be engaged to a peer who was on his deathbed, thought it was a stroke of good fortune, because she "might be a widow in a very short time, and not be troubled long with him."[20]

But in case you are getting any ideas where this might be leading, it was considered high treason for a woman to be caught plotting to kill her husband, punishable by being burned alive. It seemed that if you lived in medieval or early Renaissance Europe, your best bet would be to marry young to a rich old fellow with a bad heart condition, and faithfully feed him double bacon cheeseburgers and light his cigarettes for him. As I understand it, that still works, but people seem to frown on it today. Back then, you would be applauded for your success when he keeled over, just like you would be applauded today for having your startup tech company go public.

Housekeepers and Lovers

Hey, little girl, comb your hair, fix your make-up.
Soon he will open the door.
Don't think because there's a ring on your finger
You needn't try any more.
For wives should always be lovers, too.
Run to his arms the moment he comes home to you.
I'm warning you.
Day after day, there are girls at the office.
And men will always be men.
Don't send him off with your hair still in curlers.
You may not see him again.

~from "Wives and Lovers," by
Burt Bacharach & Hal David, 1963

By the dawn of the 18th century, social changes were taking place that began to change the nature of women's roles, rights, and their economic position, and the accepted function of marriage. First, the industrial revolution changed the world and society forever. The spread of wage labor gave the working class greater economic freedom, but debased the economic value of "women's work." It usurped the power held by those with land and titles, putting it instead into the hands of industrialists.

The "bottom line" turned the social order upside down and took away a titled woman's value as a connection in the old landed gentry system. Crass money became king, and those who could earn it became the new courtiers of wealth.

Prior to the industrial revolution, a middle class or working class wife ran the household like a CFO (Chief Financial Officer). She took care of resources, did charity work, ran the operations of farm or business, and oversaw the general domestic needs of the family. The actual grunt work—scrubbing the floors, cooking, washing dishes, feeding the pigs, and all those not-so-fun (and laborious) activities—were done by servants. Only the poorest of families did not have servants to take care of the more mundane chores of the household.[21]

But in the new economy, this all changed. The industrial revolution changed the world and society forever. Men began working in factories and offices away from the home, and their productive lives became less involved in the family. As men became the primary breadwinners, money began to flow differently into the family, and wives lost what little financial power they had previously had. The home became less a place of production and an economic center, and more of a place of refuge for the hardworking man who came home weary and hungry at the end of the day.[22]

Wives found themselves demoted from CFO to housekeeper, cook, and nursemaid. After all, someone had to do the child-rearing, cooking and cleaning, and if the wife wasn't needed to run the large household, farm or business, it made sense for her to save money by firing the servants and doing the maids' work herself.[23]

Second, the idea of the love-based marriage began to gain momentum. By the late 17th century, men and women had begun to have a say in the choice of their mates, and since sexual attraction and affection matter more to teenagers than money, status, and security do, kids threw caution to the wind and began to dream of marriage as a union of lovers rather than a political and business merger.[24]

The wife subsequently became, not a business partner, someone whose skills complemented the work of her husband, but a separate and new entity, the "heart" of the family, and her job was to make life more enjoyable for her breadwinner husband and to care for the children. She was responsible for being the emotional and moral center, and later, to be a good sexual partner, catering to her husband's fantasies.[25] As the role of children changed from that of economic assets, capable of working and earning an income for the family, to economic dependents, the role of wife as mother and lover began to emerge as the preferred image over the image of wife as family CFO.

Consequently, in the 18th, 19th, and even 20th centuries, women found themselves less, not more of an economic force. Their roles and work were considered less valuable than men's because the men were earning actual cash wages. Women's work, although demanding, earned nothing, and so homemakers were absolutely dependent upon their husbands financially.

Interestingly, the law saw their vulnerability and evolved to reflect the new ideal of stay-at-home mom and wage-earner father. Women were encouraged both socially and legally to become housewives rather than wage-earners. Marriage and divorce laws, originally favorable to men, now protected wives and children if husbands abandoned their families. Even women who were not legally married enjoyed the protection of "common law" marriage.[26]

This model became the new "ideal" marriage. It reached its height of acceptance in the middle of the last century, where the "perfect" family consisted of a hard-working man who left home each day to go to the office or factory, and the mom, who stayed home, baked cookies, and vacuumed the living room while wearing heels and pearls. The children went to school and played in the yard rather than working the fields or serving an apprenticeship. The Cleavers' time had come.

These were good times, at least for white, married, middle class women in the developed world. I do not mean to turn a blind eye to the plight of minorities and the poor, who still suffered from economic and social hardships.

The seeds of their discontent were already germinating underneath the sheen of middle class America and would eventually cause upheaval. But for now, for the mainstream majority, things were comfortable: the economy was perking along very nicely, wages were high, taxes were low, and so was inflation. A single wage earner was able to support a family, and new, labor saving household devices like vacuum cleaners, washers and dryers, and indoor plumbing were becoming commonplace in Western households. Housewives found they had time to break away from the constant chores of running a home to engage in more fun, social activities. In America especially, bridge clubs and book clubs sprang up like daffodils on an April day.

A man's success was measured by how well he was able to support his family, and men often bragged about having "high maintenance" wives. Boys from respectable families often declared, "No wife of mine will ever work," and girls were conditioned by the norms of the day to be glad to hear it.

Of course, many women found this way of life limiting. If you want to see the downside of living in a comfortable, but constraining nest, look at some of the old episodes of "I Love Lucy." The show was designed to illustrate the foibles of a ditzy woman who is foolish enough to want to have a career of her own as an entertainer, despite the fact that her husband provides a good living for her (and there is that small obstacle of her lack of talent). But I find Lucy a study in frustration. Clearly, taking care of the Ricardo household does not feed Lucy's soul. She yearns for a life far bigger than the easy, affluent, superficial one that she has.

The Battle of the Sexes

Q: When does a woman care for a man's company?
A: When he owns it.

The breadwinner husband/dependent wife model for the family remained unchallenged into the 1960s, as the economy continued to be strong enough to support a single wage-earner household. But change was beginning to roil even as the halcyon period of the late 40s and 50s was at its crest. Contrary to popular misconception, the first people to become disgruntled with the situation were not feminists, but men. Women seemed to be having all the fun. Marriage meant more responsibility for men, less for women.

In 1953, Hugh Hefner founded *Playboy* magazine to raise a cry against male family responsibilities. From the beginning, the publication encouraged men to "enjoy the pleasures the female has to offer without becoming emotionally involved," or financially responsible. An article in the first issue of *Playboy,* titled "Miss Gold Digger of 1953," implied that women were on the prowl for men to support them. Hefner's ideas caught on *fast.* By 1956, the magazine was selling more than one million copies per month.[27]

The battle of the sexes was on, as evidenced by popular entertainment of the period. Movies in the late '50s and '60s featured swinging bachelors whose sole purpose was to seduce beautiful women, and beautiful women who were trying to "trap" men into marriage. The hard-drinking, dangerous living, womanizing James Bond became a hero. Movie heroines lost their moral toughness and turned into sex kittens.

Marriage laws began to shift away from the role of protecting women and their children. Sadly, many women got caught in the transition during the late 20th century. They married under one set of rules, where they thought they would be taken care of and loved until death, and were divorced under quite another. Cheating husbands frequently got the best end of the deal, and divorcees who were once comfortable wives, ended up impoverished. Women began to grumble, and the next thing you know, they were burning their bras in the streets and demanding equal pay. Women returned to the workforce in numbers by choice and by tough circumstances, but laws and tradition still prevented them from having an equal footing—or equal pay—with men.

Still, women managed to circumvent bad laws and bad customs. In the early '60s my family had a friend from India named Niru. She had a full time job that her husband (now ex-husband) knew about. She also had a part time job he did not know about. Because he had a long commute, and both her jobs were in the immediate neighborhood, she managed to start early at her first job, then run to the other, and she got home just in time to throw dinner in the oven and sit down at her knitting before her husband arrived. He was a bit of a bully: Niru was of a lower caste, and he never let her or their children forget it. He controlled the finances and saved the money she made that he knew about in order to bring his parents from India to live in the U.S. He also spent a good bit on himself and sent lavish gifts back home to his relatives.

Niru saved the money he didn't know about in order to get her own parents here from India. She also saved money she was able to skim off the grocery budget, the clothing allowance, the home maintenance account, and so forth. As you may imagine, her parents moved here years before his did. Niru is now happily married to her second husband who has no pretensions about his caste, or hers. She still keeps a little stash set aside, just in case.

The economy began deteriorating by the late 1960s: tax rates increased, inflation reared its head, and it became harder for a single breadwinner to keep a family afloat. Family law and conventional custom became even less benign to women, working or not, and to mothers. Women were universally considered less able to handle money than men. In the US, employed, married women had a difficult time getting credit at all if their husbands did not work.[28] When my aunt was divorced in the '60s, one of the first pieces of mail she received as a newly free woman was a notice that her department store credit cards were being revoked. Even though she had money of her own, the store figured she would be too irresponsible to use it well. They weren't taking any chances!

Nobody was shocked by that back then, aside from my fiercely feminist mother who promptly marched down to the local bank and demanded a loan in her name just on principle. She got it, but I think she may have signed my father's name. As keeper of the family finances, she considered it her right—and responsibility—to deal with all things pertaining to money. She endorsed Dad's paychecks, wrote checks and signed his name, took out credit cards in his name that he never bothered to look at. My mother was fortunate in her choice of a husband because he indulged her desire for financial control, despite what the law said. The sad fact was that women of all economic situations were routinely denied credit and wage equality, and hardly anybody blinked an eye.

Still, the "ideal" situation of getting married and becoming the glamorous, loving wife of a man who earned enough money to keep her and the family comfortable while she stayed home to "play house" with the children presented a pretty picture to many a girl, and it continued to shimmer as a golden standard to which many aspired during the '70s,

'80s and '90s. Many men and women both still see it as the "traditional" way of life, despite the fact that it existed only in a very small corner of history and the world, and came about only as a result of a specific set of economic and social circumstances. In its various stages of evolution, our idea of the "traditional" family lasted only about 250 years, or about 4.5% of the time since the dawn of civilization.

Change continued at an increasing pace. By the end of the 20th century, women had become a permanent fixture in the workforce, not just because economic circumstance generally demand that women earn an income, but also because women have rediscovered that they happen to *like* working. They enjoy being productive, and now that all careers are open to them, and their average income has nearly matched that of men's, they have begun to hit their stride.[29] They still are less likely to work a full-time schedule and are more likely to leave the labor force for longer periods of time than men to raise children or help with aging parents. However, I think it's safe to say that the Cleavers have retired.

The Practical Sex?

Paddle Your Own Canoe
~Poem title by Sarah Bolton, 1853

In some ways, things have come full circle, or more aptly, have come to a higher point in an ascending spiral. Women are more frequently than not, wage earners. We own and run businesses. We are allowed, by law and by custom, to take charge of our own finances and the finances of not only the family, but of corporations and governments.

But we still have a way to go. Studies by the Oppenheimer Mutual Fund family have found that middle class women today feel less financially secure than men do. Unlike the Roman women of the 4th century, BC, they are less likely to believe they can handle money well, and unlike the ladies of medieval Europe, they are more likely to be concerned that they might face a poverty-stricken old age. In some ways they have lost confidence in their ability to make their future comfortable and secure. I believe a part of their fear is due to a loss of self-confidence stemming from a loss of *self-awareness*.

Women are rapidly learning how to make money, but they haven't gotten comfortable with what that really means. Rather than being glad that they now have another resource to add to their arsenal of resources, they have allowed their reliance on money to usurp the value of all their other, older, innate resources. They have begun to buy into the notion that money is wealth and money is security and money is what it takes to make good things happen, and if they lack money, they will surely fail.

In reality, it isn't money that is the beginning of all good things. Rather, it is the self, the strength, the intelligence, the wherewithal to create anything and everything

Deborah Griffitts Hining

worth having. It's the stuff we are made of that will help us acquire the stuff of living. In order to go forward, we should look backward and inward, learning from our foremothers and trusting our instincts.

According to Niall Ferguson in *The Ascent of Money*, after decades of studies, there is a growing consensus that women are better credit risks than men are, and that good money management may actually be a distinctly female trait.[30] That's right, ladies, it's in the intact double X chromosome. And in the larger mass of "white matter" in our brains, which connects reason and feeling and makes us understand that what we do now will make a difference in how we feel later.[31]

And perhaps it's also in the functioning mammaries. We understand that an outflow of calcium and calories cannot exceed intake without there being serious consequences. We know that if we are to feed the baby, we have to give our bodies an extra gallon of butter pecan ice cream with fudge sauce, just as we know we can't spend more money than we bring home.

When we have control of the family budget, we can be remarkably stingy in order to make sure our families are well cared for. We will figure out a way to pay for ballet lessons and the band uniforms for the children, even if we have to sell Tupperware door to door or make a completely different dinner four nights a week from canned peas, mac and cheese, and a few leftovers. We know how to clip coupons and where the sales are. We mend, we bake, we salvage and trade, and we know how to stretch a dollar so thin you can see through it. We are not afraid to ask for help or reluctant to give help when it is needed. We make do.

And, if we go to the trouble to learn how to do it, we make better investors. We are less emotional when it comes to buying and selling securities, and therefore less likely to buy high and sell low. We do not see investing as competition, as men often do, constantly seeking out the "hot" stocks of the week, but as a means to long-term security. The portfolio of an informed woman is generally less volatile and better diversified than that of an equally informed man.[32]

In some parts of the world where the despair of poverty lies rank in the air, social scientists and economists have discovered that giving communities a leg-up by loaning people money to establish small businesses helps to build hope, and even prosperity. Entire communities have been lifted out of misery due to these small loans to entrepreneurs. After years of research and experimentation in blighted areas, lenders now know that the best people to give such loans to are women.

Women, even poor, uneducated ones, have consistently proven themselves better credit risks than men. They are more likely to use the money they borrow to actually establish and profitably run businesses, and they make their payments on schedule. Men in these poorer communities, it has been discovered, are more inclined to spend their wages, and sometimes extra money they borrow, on alcohol, gambling, and other vices than they do on loan repayments.[33] The citizens of Lydia already proved that disparity in inclinations long ago when women set up their brothels and earned their independence by selling sex to men.

Throughout Africa, except in Muslim communities where women are still subject to repressive laws, almost all market business is conducted by women, and has been for centuries. The women carry produce to market, negotiate, buy and sell. The exchange system is relaxed, with trading and bartering taking place in a casual atmosphere of common goodwill. Business relationships are built on the more personal relationships of kinship and friendship.[34]

Deborah Griffitts Hining

That makes sense. Where did you find your hair stylist or your dermatologist? Chances are, you asked your girl-friend who she uses, and you probably have referred some of your service providers to your friends. Shoot, you probably *are* a friend to your service providers. My best friends are my clients, and for good reason. The act of taking care of people builds feelings of goodwill toward them, and that is a biological fact as well as an emotional one. Nurturing behavior releases oxytocin, which is one of the "feel good" hormones linked to bonding in females. It's a simple fact that we tend to like the people we do things for.[34]

We have the advantage in other ways as well. Being naturally less competitive than men, we tend to be more aware that our value lies not in how much we have, but in what we do and in our personal relationships. Yet, once we have made up our minds about what's important to us, we don't let anything stand in our way of them. Lord help the person who molests a baby bear when her mother is around, and Lord help anyone who stands between us and that butter pecan ice cream with fudge sauce when we have a nursing child around. Once we definitely set our minds to do something, it generally happens.

Finally, because women have had the advantage of traditionally NOT having control of money, we have developed a knack for getting along without it and for finding interesting and creative ways to acquire what is necessary to us in other ways. In the past, women were not so concerned with the procurement of wealth as an emblem of power and did not give it undue significance.

Rather, they treated money as a tangible resource, like any other resource they could use to make their lives more comfortable. They used their ability to persuade and their social currency and skills to circumvent the limits imposed upon them. We still have the ability to do that, but in our newly acquired affluence, we sometimes find ourselves being distracted and forgetting some very important things. Now we need to get back to basics and figure out only two things, just as our ancestresses did:

1. What we *really* want

2. What resources to use to get it.

Read on!

CHAPTER 2

LIVING WELL IN A
PLACE OF PLENTY
(of distractions)

It's pretty hard to tell what does bring happiness.
Poverty and wealth have both failed.
~Frank McKinney Kin Hubbard
(American humorist, writer)

What Women (and Men) Want

In 1904, Bessie Anderson Stanley shared the secret to
a successful life with her grandson, the Rev. Arthur Stanley
Harvey: "Live well, laugh often, love much." That resonates
with a lot of people, including me. I have permanently glued
up wooden block letters on my dining room wall that spell
that out, with a slight addition: "Live Well ~ Laugh Often ~
Pray Hard ~ Love Much."

I believe that if we all lived by that simple creed, the
whole world would be a lot better off. Too bad it's not easy
to figure out how to actually do that. We know what laughing,
praying, and loving mean, but the notion of "living well" is
a bit slippery. What did Bessie mean by it?

Did she mean we should be successful at what we do,
have wealth, just be content? While all these things are nice,
there is more to "living well." There is another, higher state
where we find life not just is nice, but truly meaningful and
good. While Bessie called that state "living well," others
might call it "fulfillment" or living "joyfully." Psychologist

Abraham Maslow coined the terms "self-actualization" and "transcendence" to describe it.

There is a difference between merely feeling content with life and living well. Generally, we are content when we have fulfilled basic physical and psychological needs, such as being safe, warm, and fed, and when we feel loved. We need to feel that we belong to a group or family who regards us with esteem and affection. We also want freedom, serenity and peace, to understand things, and to be surrounded by enough beauty to make life pleasant.

Self-actualization, transcendence, fulfillment—truly living well—is more difficult. That state requires that we feel that our own needs are adequately met so that we are free to reach out to tend to the needs of others. We also find it when we are completely absorbed with activities that energize us, when we are so engaged in our work that we lose sense of ourselves and of time. We reach our full potential when these are combined with a sense of moral purpose, when we are connected and aware of our blessings, when we know that our lives are meaningful.

Home of the Brave or Land of the Needy?

One would think that in this land of freedom and plenty, where we live, we all should be living well. If you are affluent enough to have bought this book, you probably are in an economic class that doesn't have to worry about starvation or death from exposure. Most of us are blessed with the liberty to choose our life paths. We can love whomever we wish. We have educational resources so we can pursue our interests.

But like many middle class Westerners, we frequently find ourselves just a little dissatisfied with the state of our lives. Why is that? Why do we, in spite of the fact that we are warm and well fed, still hunger? Why do we feel the need to spend much of our lives acquiring things when we already have more material goods than 90% of the rest of the world?

The answer is simple, but not easy. Despite our relative wealth, many of us have not fulfilled all of our basic human needs to our full satisfaction. While very few of us in the West need more material things, the unfulfillment of many of our emotional and spiritual needs causes us to feel that we should do more or have more. No matter how much we have acquired in the way of stuff, or education, or things of beauty, and even if we feel loved and important, many of us continue to hunger for something else. That yearning prevents us from reaching our full potential.

I believe that in many ways, our very affluence prevents us from living well by distracting us from understanding what we really need. In order to fulfill our basic psychological need of feeling a part of a society or group, we feel we must measure up to the standards the society sets. Because we are a part of a very affluent society, we, and everybody else, can afford to buy an awful lot (and there is an awful lot to buy, thanks to the miracles of technology) and do more than ever before.

And now we have come to believe that we *should* buy more and do more. It's easy to become dissatisfied with the same old stuff when we are constantly made aware that others have more than we do. As a result, we keep raising our standards of what we should have in the way of consumer items and leisure activities, and we spend our energies constantly seeking out and pursuing these things.

Economists Betsey Stevenson and Justin Wolfers have recently established that there is a high correlation between the wealth of a nation and the happiness of its citizens, and as nations become relatively richer, the people

Deborah Griffitts Hining

become correspondingly happier. There is one significant exception, however. Despite the fact the United States is much more affluent today than it was in the 1970s, with a general higher standard of living for all, American women have actually reported themselves less happy today than they were in the 1970s.

In an interview with *Boston Globe*, Stevenson and Wolfers surmise that one of the possible explanations for this decline in happiness is that American women may be judging their happiness against a new frame of reference. "Women may be assessing their happiness with greater expectations for their lives and are more likely to feel that they have come up short."[1]

As we grow wealthier, we expect to grow wealthier still. As we become accomplished, we expect ourselves to become even more accomplished. When I was working on my PhD, one of my best friends, whom I adore and thought she had it all together in every way, commented that she thought she ought to get a graduate degree. Why? Because all her friends were getting advanced degrees. I thought I was taking the easy way by staying in school as long as I could, while she was the brave one who actually was earning her own living. Yet, she felt left behind because she didn't have letters after her name.

Apparently, her feeling of inadequacy is quite common among American women today, and we pay a high price as we try to compensate. Stevenson and Wolfers noted that American women's relative unhappiness today might also be due to the fact that increased "financial gains for women might have been offset by greater emotional and mental strain."[2] Ya think? How demanding is it to work at a job which keeps the family looking successful, and at the same time keep the babies dry and fed, be the social director, a sexy hottie, and emotional center of the family—*and then* expect yourself to continually accomplish more? Sheesh. I know you're a woman, but nobody can pile on that much and still feel chipper.

This "greater emotional and mental strain" we are subjecting ourselves to is causing millions of us to suffer from a malady endemic to the 21st century called "adrenal fatigue," according to naturopathic doctor James Wilson. When the adrenal glands are chronically overly exerted because we live with constant stress, they stop functioning properly, and this can cause harm to every organ and system in our bodies. Dr. Wilson and many others believe that adrenal fatigue is responsible for exacerbating or causing such problems as allergies, arthritic pain, decreased immune response, depression, memory loss, insomnia, low sex drive, premenstrual tension, and increased difficulty during menopause.

Unchecked, it can lead to chronic respiratory infections, fibromyalgia, chronic fatigue syndrome, hypoglycemia, diabetes, autoimmune disorders, alcoholism, and even cancer. [3]

Not only does constant stress ruin our health, it also can make us fat. Excess secretions of cortisol, one of the stress hormones, causes belly fat to accumulate, so that someone suffering from this syndrome actually changes body shape, becoming more rotund.[4] Yeah, like we need that. But it seems that we are constantly asking for it, and we are condemning our children to suffer it as well.

If you are in your 20s or 30s, grew up middle class and went to college, your growing up experience was no doubt busier and more affluent than your parents' or grandparents' experiences. If you have young children, they are probably getting used to a busier and more "accessorized" lifestyle than you had. As a child, I played neighborhood baseball in the vacant lot next door. My kids had a Nintendo, took dance classes and played organized sports. Their kids will probably start out with a Wii and an I-phone, and run from one set of lessons taught by professionals to another. They will be smarter, busier, more accomplished, and breathless with activity.

Our lives are not easier, despite our labor saving devices. The pressures today are different and much more intense. All of us work harder to do the things we want to do or think we should do because popular culture does its damndest to make us feel inferior if we aren't able to keep up with the higher social, material, and professional standards we set for ourselves.

I didn't work much during my college years, and didn't need much spending money. My friends and I lived on campus, ate in the college cafeterias, and didn't need a car because we didn't go anywhere. Entertainment consisted of attending ball games, singing in the school chorus, and hanging out in the dorms. We had fun. I never felt deprived: in fact, I felt that I had a great, even luxurious life. There wasn't a lot of pressure to do anything other than make decent grades and maybe splurge on a movie at the student center now and then.

Now college kids work 20-40 hours per week in order to make enough money to pay their car insurance and spend Spring Break on a cruise or in a bar on the beach in some exotic country. They have been told that they must have at least one semester abroad, and an internship at a major corporation, or their resumes will be inadequate.

We are under greater pressure to conform to lives of more and more consumption and complication. Keeping up with the Joneses never was so difficult. You may come from a working class family, but some of your friends come from more affluent families, and they might make you believe you are missing out if you can't join them on the ski trip to Vail or Switzerland they are planning this winter. So what do you do? You work overtime or take a second job or go into debt in order to strap on those skis and risk your neck on the Black Diamond slope, not because you really love skiing, but because if you don't, you might lose the emotional benefit of your friends thinking you are cool.

More affluence means more stuff to buy, and some of the "more stuff" to buy are TVs and access to more cable channels. More cable channels means more time in front of the TV, where retailers push hard to sell even more stuff. The 2007 A.C. Nielsen survey revealed that the average child in America sees 20,000 thirty-second commercials (*167 hours!*) per year,[5] all of which shout a "Buy!" message. And not just a "Buy!" message. It's also a "Want!" or even "Need!" message, because if advertisers can't make us want things, they can't make us buy them.

As a result, advertisers and manufacturers have worked hard honing their skills, figuring out how to convince us that consumer items will meet not only our physical, but also our deepest psychological needs. And they know that our need for acceptance and belonging is so great that we can be manipulated into almost anything if we can be made to believe it will help us fit in or gain esteem.

The Basics: Food, Love, Beauty, Clothes, More Clothes, Jewelry, a Trip to Cancun. . .

Our "basic needs" consist of the essentials for physical and emotional life, but our notion of "basic" is expanding. Sure, we need a coat to stay warm. But now, one coat is not enough. We need to have five in order to withstand the brutal winter. A single pretty necklace used to suffice for ornamentation for women in centuries past. How many pretty necklaces do you own? I probably own three dozen pairs of earrings, and my daughter has even more. And of course, we "need" every single pair. We don't wear the old ones often—discreet little studs are no longer in fashion. We have to have danglies. Next year we probably will need bold, big studs, and danglies will be so last year.

Fashion magazines tell us that if we wear anything that is "out of style," others will look down on us. To our discredit, when we see someone wearing, or doing, or even thinking something that is currently unfashionable, we sometimes are guilty of looking down on her. That is too bad, because it means that we have fallen into the trap of thinking that certain material possessions or "correct" behavior or attitudes makes people more worthy of love and goodwill.

When is the last time looking down on someone made you really joyful? What? Did you say "Never?" Funny how that works. By placing so much emphasis on what is "fashionable" or "correct," we prevent ourselves from gaining what we really need—enough love, tolerance, self-confidence, a sense of belonging, peace and goodwill—to be able to claim a life well lived. [6]

My former paraplanner, Julie, is one of those creative, constantly cheerful people who immediately connects with others and makes every encounter a party. She radiates goodwill and an easy confidence, despite the fact that she buys all her clothes on the discount rack or at the Goodwill. She is very frugal because she is paying off student loans and looking forward to getting an MBA.

Once, when visiting a friend in Chicago, she was out with a group of people she had just met, and in the group was a girl who tried to ingratiate herself by talking about the Fendi bag she was going to get on sale for a mere $1400. When Julie responded by laughing about her own thrift store purse, the girl began denigrating her and her inability to buy nice things.

Now, I'm guessing that this girl talked about her Fendi bag only because she had little else to say. Being obsessed with "things," she wasn't very interesting, but probably believed that if she dropped a name and belittled someone who was not affluent, she would be more attractive to others. The funny thing is, the more she flaunted her things, the more everyone unfavorably compared her misguided attempts to gain acceptance with the genuine goodwill that Julie created.

> As this book goes to publication, Julie is beginning her second semester at Tulane's prestigious MBA program, on scholarship. As it turns out, money was no object!

Psychologists agree that people who are most concerned with money and possessions are consistently less happy than those who are not." Research psychologist Ed Diener goes so far as to say, "Materialism is toxic for happiness."[7]

This unhappy girl had bought into the myth perpetuated by the mass consumer market that stuff or exotic or glamorous activities can make us more fulfilled, more loved, and more admired. Advertisements are designed to make a connection between what's for sale and the deep desires that we all have. It's easy to see how material things can fulfill some of our more basic needs like food, clothing, shelter, and so forth. But commercials also contrive to create a link between objects and our higher emotional needs such as love, security, and respect. Sadly, the relationship between objects and respect or love can work in some circles in the short term, but in the long run, it proves hollow.

"Buy this security system and your family will be safe," makes some sense, but "Buy this perfume and the most awesome guy will fall in love with you," butchers logic. Nevertheless, the mere possibility that perfume will lead to love or that a security system will really make you secure appeals to us on such a deep level that we automatically respond in a positive way.

Some commercials even try to make us believe that some things can help us become self-actualizing or transcendent: "Buy this dog food and we'll give a portion of proceeds to the animal shelter. You will prove yourself a more moral person." "Buy a ticket for this cruise and your spirit will soar."

Really good advertising campaigns have a way of creating a need in people where no need has existed before. I know from experience how effective they can be. Until just a few years ago, I had no idea I had yellow teeth. But then I saw an ad for a product that whitens teeth. Imagine that! The pictures proved how ugly, yellow teeth could be magically transformed with a few easy treatments with this amazing product. The next thing I knew, I was grimacing in the mirror, examining my sad, yellow teeth, and I came to the startling realization that I *needed*—couldn't live without—that tooth whitening product!

Not only that, I have also discovered the horrible truth that I have cellulite on my thighs and my eyelashes are too short and my hair is dull. I wear the wrong clothes, my wrinkles are unattractive, and my shoes are going out of style. Here I was, blithely skipping through life, unaware that I needed so much help, until I got cable television and began paying attention to commercials.

Of course, I'm half joking here. Many consumer items do make our lives better, and I have to say, I am happier looking in the mirror when I see a set of pearly whites flashing back at me. I don't mean to imply that we should refrain from buying things that make our lives easier or better, if we can afford them. Some things please our aesthetic sensibilities and make life more fun. As a matter of fact, I would like it better if people in general made a greater effort to look more pleasing to all of us. I think we owe it to the world to make it as pretty as we can with our appearance and with our attitudes.

We just need to firmly understand that while longer eyelashes and white teeth might make us more beautiful according to the standards of our society, being more beautiful doesn't automatically mean we will be more loved and respected, happier, or more fulfilled. In fact, it could have the opposite effect. Many beautiful women feel hounded, not loved. Some "successful," wealthy people surround themselves with luxury, but do not have a true friend.

Our constant race for doing more, being more, having more makes us both unhappy and unhealthy, and it limits one of our most important resources. According to Jerome Kagan from his research at Harvard University, excessive cortisol not only makes us fat, it also limits our capacity to make the emotional bond we create with others though facial expressions. Because it causes greater muscle tension, our faces become less visibly responsive to others[8] when we are under stress, and less responsiveness means a weaker connection and less social currency.

Deborah Griffitts Hining

If It's Not New, It's Not in Fashion
~on a Billboard I saw in Chicago—honest!

The manufacturers of material goods, with the help of the media, deliberately manipulate trends and the tastes of our culture. They make fashions come and go, and make us change and re-change our sense of style so that we will constantly dump the old in favor of the new.

Men used to fantasize about the curve of a woman's belly and a plump, soft bottom. Girdles came into being not because women wanted to look like they had sexy, flat tummies and desirably tight rear-ends, but in order to be more modest. A rounded tummy and jiggly butt were too hot to be seen in polite company. It would be like not putting a bra on your double D girls and wearing a thin t-shirt at the office today—men just wouldn't get any work done at all, and your name might end up scribbled on the bathroom wall.

> In the 1959 movie, *Anatomy of a Murder*, about a man on trial for killing a man who raped his wife, Jimmy Stewart (the defense attorney) keeps telling Lee Remick (the rape victim) to wear a girdle to the courtroom. He makes the point that she looks too sexy without it, and the jury might think she invited the rape.

Now, a belly on a woman looks gross, and I *really* need an Abdomenociser. And I'd better act soon. If I order in the next 10 minutes I can get the bonus of a carrying case and a special workout video. Hot dog! Where's my credit card? I'm going to look fabulous! My husband will fall at my feet and worship me, and my girlfriends will be oh, so jealous!

Intellectually, we know we can't buy love and belonging, success, or fulfillment, but we also understand that we can buy objects that look like symbols of these values—objects which seem to "prove" that we are fulfilled and living well. While in reality, there may be a huge gap between the symbol and the real thing, our culture has somehow come to value symbols almost as much as the real thing. If your boyfriend buys you a three carat diamond ring, it doesn't necessarily mean that he's devoted to you, nor does it necessarily mean that he is brilliantly successful, although your friends may be convinced that he does and is. How many carets of bling did Tiger Woods buy Elin? How many did Bernie Madoff buy Ruth? There is a definite connection sometimes between love and beautiful gifts, between a show of wealth and living well, and we want to believe that because such a connection flows from one direction, it also flows from the other.

Indeed, we often accept the notion that the trappings of success and the outward manifestations of happiness can actually lead to success and happiness. There is even a mantra for the phenomenon: "Fake it till you make it," meaning that if you dress for success, buy the right car, and the right house in the right neighborhood, eventually your reality will catch up with appearances. You can even make yourself happy by putting on a show of happiness.

Unfortunately, when we succumb to the lie that we can make it by faking it enough, our lives become mere pretense, not real. Fake morality? Happiness? Self-Actualization? I don't think so. You can't be authentically happy, moral, and self-actualizing if you are just pretending. Believe it or not, you can be a caring person without buying that special dog food. Your actions would be more authentically moral if you volunteer at the animal shelter yourself. You may want to buy a security system to keep your children safe, but that is only one of many things you should do. More importantly, you should do other things to help maintain their safety, like being there every night to watch over their computer use, making them wear seat belts, keeping sharp objects out of their way, locking the door, and so forth. You have to be actually involved in your family's activities, giving your own time and your own energy: in other words, part of your own self. The only currency you can use to buy yourself a life well lived is your own heart, mind, body, and soul. Money is essentially worthless.

Retail Therapy: Shortcut To A Dead End

I know that buying stuff can temporarily cure a lot of emotional ills. It isn't called "retail therapy" for nothing. Let's face it, many of us have turned a bad day into a pretty good one because we ran out and bought something fabulous, and that temporary balm feels good to a bruised ego or heart. Bad day at work? Go shopping. It will make you feel better. Boyfriend dump you? Go shopping. It will ease the heartache. Have a falling out with your best friend? Go shopping. You'll buy something that makes her green with envy, and *that* will make you feel good.

I fall prey to that temptation more than I care to admit, because it's easier to go shopping than it is to do what it would take to really make me feel lastingly better. Buying something takes less energy than volunteering at the soup kitchen, spending an hour in prayer, calling an estranged friend to work things out. All that sounds too much like work. When I'm blue or angry, I don't feel particularly in-clined to do something self-sacrificing or charitable. I just want to consume something to fill *me* up, to concentrate on and pamper me, Me, *ME*!

Retail therapy is the strategy we might employ by default, although we know that the buzz we get from shopping wears off very quickly. The thrill of making the perfect purchase lasts for only a moment—ok, in the case of a really fantastic pair of earrings that you got at 75% off, maybe it lasts for a couple of days or weeks. But the more pairs of "fantastic" earrings you accumulate, the shorter the duration of the shopping high.

You'd think that we would learn that these highs are so short lived that it's hardly worth the effort, never mind the expense. But we don't because it's too much trouble to think about it when we are feeling needy. We want to take the path of least resistance. And we have no reason to curb our spending. We are so affluent that it doesn't hurt us (or so we think) when we blow ten or 100 bucks on something we really don't need.

Buying things for ourselves because we believe those things will make us fulfilled ultimately not only does not work, it actually hurts us because the more we accumulate, and the more we become addicted to the shopping high, the more difficult it is to let go of the stuff so that we can reach for what we really need. We don't end up happier or more satisfied or self-actualized. We just end up with an armful of fancy bags that are labeled with something like "FAMILY CLOSENESS" or "SUCCESS" in big, glittery letters, but which are actually completely empty.

And sometimes, because we want to believe that these bags really do contain something worthwhile (since we have gone to the effort and expense to obtain them), we begin to believe that having those sparkly bags is very important. Never mind that they don't contain the things they claim to

Deborah Griffitts Hining

contain. We just love them because they are pretty and they have the right label.

They also are easier to obtain than the real thing is. In our affluence, it is easier to buy a facsimile of respect, love, or family harmony, than to actually work for them. And when we fall in love with—and pursue—these empty, glittering, well-labeled bags, we sometimes forget how hard we need to work for the important things.

How many times do children have serious problems because their parents gave them "things" rather than the love they really need? Studies published by the Journal of *Marriage and Family*, and others, have established that the best way to give young girls self-esteem and to keep them from becoming sexually active too early is for their fathers to give them plenty of cuddling and love, even through their teen years.[9]

That makes sense: if snuggling on her daddy's lap provides a girl with all the necessary nurturing and bonding fixes she needs, she is less likely to try to get them sleeping with the adolescent boys on the football team. So how come really well educated, loving dads give their little girls money to go shopping, but don't take the time to lie in the back yard with them on a summer night and point out the constellations?

Because they're too busy. They got sidelined chasing after their own perceived needs—grabbing at the empty bags labeled "Esteem," "Belonging," " The Good Life." It takes energy to fight that, energy they don't have because they used it all up chasing the glitter. And to make things worse, they pass along the message that those empty bags are the means to happiness every time they open their wallets rather than their arms.

It's time we separated the idea of "living well" from "affluence." Living well is not difficult, even on a budget.

If you have to buy your purses, and all your other clothes and accessories at a consignment shop, or if you consider a car "new" if you've just purchased it, and it has less than 100,000 miles on it, you can still have a marvelous life.

I grew up in a working class family, but for my entire childhood, I never realized that we were not well off. I did notice that other kids wore braces on their teeth and took family vacations to far-off places (like the beach in another state), but I never really gave it much thought because I was so busy doing fun things like playing baseball with my friends, watching lightening storms, listening to my dad tell funny stories.

Looking back, I now realize that we had been living by a recipe that had been handed down in my family for generations, one that I treasure even more than I treasure my mother's recipe for pineapple upside down cake. I happily share it with you and hope you find it to be as delicious and nourishing as I have.

Recipe for the Good Life

1 cup of fun and excitement +
1 cup of beauty, less a tablespoon of stuff

Here's a test: Think really hard. What was one item you have purchased that has given you the biggest dose of long-term happiness? It should be easy because there probably are very few of them. For me, it's the classic style Thunderbird I had been wanting for decades, but never got around to buying until a couple of years ago. Sure, it's nine years old and parts fall off it every now and then, but it's a sweet little ride, and I love how I feel in it when the top is off and I'm driving under a blue and white sky.

Other than the Thunderbird, I have very few *things* that have given me lasting happiness. As a matter of fact, the only things I can think of at the moment are my house, the flowers in my garden, the bird feeders, and works of art painted by my husband, Mike, and our daughter Mary Elizabeth.

And you know what? When I look around my house, cluttered with a bunch of stuff that I once thought I needed, I find it makes me nervous. How am I going to clean all that? How much trouble will it be to box it all up when we move? What if somebody robs the house and steals it? That's valuable stuff! I need to take better care of it! Frankly, it has become a burden to me because the care and storage of it is a determining factor as I make important life decisions. How can I sell my house and move to Florence if I have to find a place to put it all while we are gone?

It is different when I think about the things I have *done* which have given me happiness. Each happy memory lives inside me like a little soap bubble, and every time I think of one, I feel it lift my heart. How about you? What is the one thing you have done (or experienced) which has given you the most lasting happiness? I bet it's harder to think of just one thing, for your list of wonderful experiences is probably very long.

A 2003 study by psychologists Leaf van Boven and Thomas Gilovich, and a separate study by Ryan Howell at San Francisco State University, show that people consistently appreciate memorable experiences more than they do physical possessions.[10] In other words, doing is better than having!

Even the Thunderbird as the *thing* is good for me only because it provides an *experience*. It makes me happy because I have had so many good times in it. The car itself is merely a vehicle that gives me the opportunity to experience beauty, freedom, fun, and often, connectedness with others.

Oh, happy me on a winding mountain road with a friend by my side, the wind in our hair and the radio blasting!

A double handful of productivity

Things really happy people are likely to say:

"Oh Boy! Monday! We get started on that new project today!"

"I woke up at 4 this morning. The solution to the problem we've been working on just popped into my head, and I got so excited about it, I came on in to work."

"I can't believe they pay me to do this."

Claremont Graduate University psychologist Mihaly Csikszentmihalyi (yes, that really is the way it's spelled. Don't ask me to pronounce it!) coined the term "flow" to describe the state when people are so engaged in absorbing activities they lose track of themselves. According to him, people who most often experience "flow," whether it happens while dishing out food at the soup kitchen or working on a new telescope to explore space, are most likely to be happy with their lives.[11] If you love what you're doing day in and day out, you love your life.

2 cups of love

One of the most important ingredients in our quest to live well is love and connection with others. Before most of us believe that we are truly living well, we feel we must be with someone we care about.

Think about a time when you were most happy. It might be a day of a spectacular snowfall or the day you graduated or the day a child was born. I'm sure there are times when you have enjoyed being alone and experiencing something wonderful, without relying on another person to share it with you, but for the most part, I bet your absolutely happiest memory has at least one other person in it.

Mike and I once spent a few days in Venice. What a beautiful city! The day we got there, the weather was perfect, the buildings sparkled in the sun, music played at every corner, the people were joyful and full of life. I walked the streets, rode in the gondolas, ate lunch at a café, watched children playing . . . and I was miserable. I had expected to spend the day in romantic bliss, but Mike was back at the hotel that day, sick with pneumonia, and he had kicked me out of our room so he could get some sleep. I had to experience one of the most romantic cities in the world in a miasma of loneliness and worry for him.

When I compare that day to the day of my 50th birthday, when Mary Elizabeth invited my closest friends to my surprise party, guess which one wins? My day in fabulous Venice doesn't hold a birthday candle to my afternoon in my own living room with my best friends.

1 pinch of gratitude +
A dash of humility

Those moments we share with loved ones that are full of adventure, beauty and fun, are like swaths of bright color over the sepia tones of our everyday existence. Not only do we enjoy them while they are happening, we also get pleasure when we remember them long after. But like *things*, the pleasures that adventures or momentary joys give us also can be short lived. They give us joy while we are engaged in them, but an excess of those without a sense of freshness and gratitude eventually can make us feel as bloated and choked as an excess of "stuff" can do.

I'll never scorn a glass of wine at a sidewalk café, or a wonderful vacation in a foreign country, or watching a Broadway musical. All these experiences are great, especially the first time we have them. New pleasures are the best because they not only are fun, but they are exciting and new.

But if you do the same fun things over and over just to consume the pleasure, you may soon stop appreciating them. Once you become jaded, you shift your paradigm—you lose perspective about what you deserve and don't deserve. You also may experience something like addiction; life is miserable if you don't get that experience frequently, even though you have ceased to really enjoy it.

After a time, the thrill is lessened, unless we deliberately heighten our senses. I'm a little less aware of the thrill in my T-bird today than I was when it was new, and I'm even irritated with it when it rains and the roof leaks. A second or third experience of something may duplicate the exact circumstances as the first, but unless we remind ourselves to be grateful for it, our perception of it changes. The moment we do something only to re-experience the pleasure, without taking into account the need to compliment it with love and gratitude, we become consumers and critics, not doers. The edges of our contentment start to get a little soft, and we are less happy than we thought we would be.

I have the extreme good fortune of being married to a man who wakes me up every morning with a cup of tea. He sits down and chats with me until I am ready to face the day. How grateful should I be for that? Yes, I am thankful, but I need to be *mindful* that I am thankful, or I will allow myself to start taking that beautiful ritual for granted.

Sometimes I wake up, and Mike's side of the bed is empty. I wait around a bit, lounging in the bed, and if he doesn't show up with my tea, I start thinking, "Where is he? Has he forgotten me? Where is my tea??? My goodness, he's late! What's wrong with him? Doesn't he know I really need my tea right now??"

Shame on me! When I start thinking that I am owed such good treatment, and he is remiss in not giving it to me, I have lost my joy in his loving nature and his willingness to do something special for me. One secret to living well is to never let yourself become so inured to a good thing that you begin to think it is your right to have it. The moment you do that, you lose the ability to live really well.[12]

Just after World War II, people reported in surveys that they were very happy — more happy than people today claim to be.[13] Why? Because they had a decent job with good wages, and they were free from the threat of danger for the first time in years. They appreciated their peace and prosperity because it was new. Now we have lived so well for so long that we think we *deserve* peace and a decent job. Ads tell us we "deserve" a good life. We "deserve" the right car, the best food, the best clothes, and now we have begun to believe it.

Do people in Bangladesh deserve less than we have? Why do we deserve the best of everything? We certainly aren't better, or smarter, or harder working. We just happen to live in a country that is so rich that good things fall in our laps. And we have reached the point where we believe we are entitled to them. Of course, that means if we don't get them, we feel shortchanged, cheated.

When we begin to believe such things, we reduce our ability to live well and fully. Discontent will prevent us from being happy with any good thing we are used to having. Our very prosperity, strength, and culture have compromised our joy that gratefulness and humility provide.

A good dollop of understanding the difference between wealth, success, and happiness

Because we have been seduced (or have seduced ourselves) into believing that having lots of good stuff gives us a good life, we extend our reasoning and assume that if we have enough of the *means* to accumulate these things, we will be fulfilled. We make the illogical leap to believing that having money, and lots of it, is the way to climb into a very good life.

Successful people, no matter what they are successful at, are generally happier, more fulfilled, and wealthier than unsuccessful people. But it isn't the wealth that causes the happiness. It isn't the success or fame that causes the fulfillment. Rather, it works the other way around. What brings success and a life well lived is simply living deliberately with love and thankfulness, consistently being engaged in doing something that fulfills you, and working toward something bigger than yourself, growing always to the next level. Involvement with other human beings, giving of yourself and your means, being productive, finding spirituality and purpose makes you rise above all small things. After that, the small, good things, including money, tend to accumulate underneath.

Socrates summed it up when he said, "Wealth does not bring about excellence, but excellence brings about wealth and all other public and private blessings."

Please note this excellence = wealth rule is not a hard and fast one. Many people who are very accomplished have chosen professions that do not give great material rewards. Their success is seen in the quality of their work, not the size of their bank accounts, and they find their happiness with what they do, despite the fact that it may earn them little. Mother Theresa, for instance, found her sense of worth and joy in picking babies off garbage heaps and giving them a decent life. There are a lot of unsung, but happy heroes out there.

Deborah Griffitts Hining

On the other side, there are many people who are very good at what they do, and are very highly compensated. They appear successful from the outside, but they are not happy with their lot in life. I would not say these people are living well. I would just call them financially well off. These are the ones who are hungry for things they cannot buy, but sometimes try to buy them anyway. They have a closet full of those glittery, empty bags, and they can't understand why they need something "more."

An open handful of sharing

After the most basic of our needs are met (purchased with money), accumulating more money does not help us to live well for the long term *unless* we learn to delight in sharing it. When we share ourselves in all ways, including our money, we begin to understand the joy of true connection. Money, and its brother, power, can be used meaningfully, but if it is not, it actually strangles our ability to find happiness. If we use money as a tool to build something good, it works well. If we fall in love with it and its ability to garner more material things or more pleasures, it becomes a monster in our lives.

Jesus wasn't kidding when he said, "The love of money is the root of all evil." Note he didn't say "Money is the root of all evil." Money is an inanimate object that has no power. Love (or lust) can be a driving force that motivates us to do things we didn't believe were possible. It's a good rule of thumb to not love anything that can't love you back. Unrequited love usually leads to misery.

We also are happiest when we are sharing ourselves. Our time and energies are two currencies that we most enjoy spending when we understand that we are making a contribution and making a difference in the lives of others.

A generous sprinkling of each:
Failure, disappointment, heartache, and setbacks

Sure, it would be great not to have to deal with any of these things, but just as you need some salt and a spoonful of bitter baking soda to make the most tasty sugar cookies, or plain old vinegar to make the best barbeque sauce, you also need disappointments to bring out the flavor of a life well lived.

I don't know anybody who is truly spoiled who is also truly happy. And as far as I'm concerned, if you haven't roundly failed at anything, you don't have many successes. Failure and setbacks mean you took risks, and they teach you to keep trying the next thing, and the next. They lead you down new paths and help remove your fear of facing new explorations. Disappointments and heartaches keep you grounded and appreciative.

A cup of acceptance

Everybody is different. You'll have more fun with them if you don't expect them to be like you and if you can delight in the differences. As I have begun to understand that more fully, I have decided to seek out people who are less inclined to consumerism than I am. I expect that they can teach me a lot about all of the above. And if I learn to accept and appreciate others who are very different from me, I not only save a lot of energy that might be spent balancing myself on that high horse, I also give my adrenal glands a rest.

Mix well and bake in a warm heart 'til done. Pray over it and enjoy with a glass of wine and some good friends, preferably in the sunshine.

Deborah Griffitts Hining

CHAPTER 3

THE ROLE OF MONEY

*Do not value money for any more nor any less than
its worth; it is a good servant but a bad master.*
~Alexandre Dumas fils, *Camille*, 1852

If you go get your car checked out, you don't care
about specifics, such as if the differential is busted or the
butterfly valve isn't functioning properly. What you really
might want to know is if the old heap can make it to California
and back so you can go to your aging aunt and uncle's 70th
wedding anniversary. You want to make sure something
doesn't happen, like the radiator exploding outside Amarillo,
Texas, leaving you stranded amid the mesquite and sage-
brush.

Ultimately, a properly functioning car has a lot to do
with the pleasure you will have at getting to this important
celebration, so you go to the trouble to take care of it. And
if you tell the mechanic you want to drive across country
and back, he will have a better understanding of what needs
to be done to it.

Money should play the same role as some mechanical
gizmo in your car. We all understand there is a very clear
relationship between money and the important things of life.
Money helps us acquire the things we need to live, just as a
sound radiator helps you get to California. But money is not
the *only* thing that helps us get the things we need or want,
just as a radiator is not the only thing you need to share in
your aunt and uncle's happiness.

In the "old" days, almost everyone lived with only the
bare necessities: they had only a few changes of clothes, a
minimum of home furnishings, and they had little money to

Deborah Griffitts Hining

spend on extras. Money was literally scarce, even for those who had abundant wealth in lands and livestock. Only a couple of centuries ago, many people made or grew most of what they needed, and they did most of their buying and selling primarily by bartering. Farmers would milk their own cows, separate out the cream, and churn it to make butter. They traded extra butter, and maybe some eggs and a bushel of wheat, for something they couldn't grow, perhaps a pound of coffee beans or the services of a miller. Money rarely crossed hands.

Some things have changed since then. First, our modern world of specialized work and an economic system based on cash (or electronic transfers) has weakened the connection between what people can do to help each other directly. We have come to depend on money as the primary, if not only, means of exchange. Even farmers work differently now. They specialize, typically growing only a few crops, and they actually have to buy the produce that other farmers grow. Dairy farmers do not churn or gather eggs for barter. They sell their raw milk to dairy processors, then go to the grocery store to buy coffee and vegetables, and maybe pasteurized milk and butter with the money they get from the sale.

Second, money has become more plentiful. The reasons for this are complicated, but to simplify, our financial system, with its new and more creative types of investments, has increased the amount of money circulating in the world's economy. The money supply grew at a rapidly increasing rate by the late 20th century with the advent of such investment vehicles as hedge funds, mortgage-backed securities, and other exotic instruments.

Not only was money literally created during that time, but now, in response to our latest financial crisis, governments are deliberately increasing the supply by issuing more bonds and cranking up the printing presses to print more money. If you want to understand this idea more fully, read Niall Ferguson's *The Ascent of Money* or Jack Weatherford's *The History of Money*. Let it suffice to say that we have much more money rattling around in our economic system today than we have had in the past.

Third, as people's working lives have become more compartmentalized and as money has become more plentiful, people have lost touch with the notion that the value of things should be related to their ability to sustain life or how much work is necessary to produce them. We now spend more on "luxuries" and proportionately less on food, basic shelter, clothing, even health care*. We can wear only so many pairs of shoes, and we can eat only so many éclairs, and after we have stuffed ourselves on those, we end up looking for, and inventing new ways to soak up the excess money. This leads us to place undue value on things with little intrinsic value, like the latest fashions or the electronic gadget of the week.

> *On Shopping.com, you can buy 100 ml of penicillin for $7. The cheapest Coach coin purse is offered for $78. The median price of an ounce of cocaine retails for $2200-$2800, according to *Narcotic News*. A standard unit of blood (about 2 cups) costs $200-$230—National Blood Data Resource Center.

The entertainment industry makes up a disproportionately large part of our economy: some sports figures, rock stars, and movie stars make hundreds of times more money than teachers, farmers, or even doctors. And this trend is accelerating. Elvis Presley died rich in 1977, but only a fraction as rich as Michael Jackson did in 2009, even taking inflation into account.

> According to *Entertainment Business*, Elvis died with a net worth somewhere between $5 million and $8 million. Michael Jackson died 32 years later with a net worth of $1 billion. If you account for inflation, Elvis' $8 million would be worth the equivalent of only $28 million or so in 2009 dollars. The real, inflation adjusted difference between the net worth of the King of Rock and Roll and the net worth of the King of Pop was about $972 million, thanks to our increasing appetite for entertainment and our skewed notion of what is valuable.

People who know how to manipulate the flow (and creation) of money can make far more than those who actually produce useable goods or life-sustaining services. You don't see any carpenters, optometrists, or physical therapists on the *Forbes'* "Richest" list. But according to *Forbes* in 2009, investment guru Warren Buffett is worth $37 billion. He's rich, not because he makes something that is of real use to people, but because he can create money out of seemingly thin air. In early pioneer America, you probably would be more likely to survive if you had the strength and skills of a hunter or trapper, but in America today, you no doubt would be better off if you know how to trade options.

The way money has evolved into a supremely important commodity has caused us to shift our perspective about its role and proper place in our lives. Although it has always been important in the civilized world, it seems to be gaining a more elevated status than ever before because we have forgotten how to live without it. We have to have it in order to survive, or, indeed, do anything at all.

It seems that money can dictate what we can do or can't do, and so it has become something of a godlike, mystical beast that wields power over the weft and weave of life. People will say they can't "afford" to do certain things like go to college or start a business. Money, or lack of it, controls both their present and their future.

At the same time, because money has become so plentiful, even during the Great Recession of '08-10, and because unnecessary consumer items have become such an important part of our culture, we are more likely to be reckless with it. When money flows easily to us because we have high-paying jobs or because it has been given to us, many times we are comfortable throwing it away or using it frivolously, even when common sense tells us we are going past the bounds of reason.

Nicholas Cage was in the news recently. Although—or maybe because—he has made tens of millions of dollars as a movie star, he is facing possible bankruptcy. It seems he bought about every shiny thing that caught his eye, including two castles and a fleet of Rolls Royces. Apparently, he didn't pay attention to how fast his bank account was dwindling.[1] You have to wonder how he could not notice!

This is not to suggest that humans have gotten badder and badder over the centuries. It's just that there is more money accessible to more people now. Certainly there have been plenty of people in the past who have been irresponsible about what they are willing to spend their money on. Historians blame much of ancient Rome's fall on the fact that the government devalued money, issued excesses of it irresponsibly, and spent too lavishly. The people got so hooked on entertainment and freebies from the government that they didn't pay attention to what their leaders were doing and allowed their country to go to pot. Several nations have gone through similar cycles.

Both of these views, that money dictates the circumstances of our lives and that money can be thrown away on frivolities, are paradigms that have pervaded—and perverted—our thinking.

I want to encourage you to put money in its proper perspective and see it as simply a valuable tool that should be used more thoughtfully, to make our own lives and the lives of others more comfortable and meaningful: to educate and to elevate, to make the world a better place. Although we have come to believe otherwise, it is no more important than other tools we use to achieve the things we want to achieve, and it can be used interchangeably with or in conjunction with those other tools.

What's Important?

The best way to mold your life as you wish it to be is not by having lots of money at your disposal. Rather, you must take the responsibility for reaching your own desires, regardless of how much or how little money you have. You must think deeply enough to understand what is truly important to you: what do you want the circumstances of your life to be? Then use whatever resources are available to you to make it happen. No one knows what you need and want better than you do, and no one is better at directing your choices to make good things happen for you. Taking responsibility is the first step to taking control.

Years ago, when I was a newly minted financial planner, I had the silly notion that my job was to help people save up a big bucket of money so they could retire early and financially well off, perhaps even die rich. I had a client whose financial situation was precarious, and I was concerned about her ability to save much because her income was limited. One day she called me, and this is how the conversation went:

Cindy: Hi, I just called to tell you I want to go to Alaska to see my sister, and I'll be spending some money for a plane ticket.

Silly Me: You can't go to Alaska. You just bought that new truck and you don't have the money. You need to wait until you have saved up for it. You might get a raise soon, and you can do it then.

Cindy: But I really want to see her. She needs me right now.

Silly Me: No! You can't! You can't afford it! We just got you out of debt, and now you need to be saving for your retirement! You cannot go! I absolutely forbid it! (sound of foot stomping the floor) No way! Forget it! (more sound of foot stomping).

Cindy: I guess you're right. I don't need to be getting back into debt.

Silly Me: Good. I'm glad that's settled. Now, go to the human resources office and bump up your contributions to your retirement plan.

Two weeks later, I got a postcard from Cindy, from Alaska. She had the good sense to ignore my misguided attempt to force the "correct" choice on her. My thinking considered only money, but Cindy knew what was most important to her, and she did what she really wanted to in a sane and sensible way. She went to see her sister, but kept her promise and didn't go into debt to buy that airline ticket. Instead she scrounged around, selling some things to drum up cash, and severely restricting her spending for a while. She scoured for deals on plane fares, and found a cheap red-eye to Fairbanks. She also delayed bumping up her contributions to her retirement plan by a few months, but in the grand scheme of things, that didn't make much of a difference.

I have to say, when I got that postcard, I felt pretty silly, but at least I had the good grace to laugh and learn from my folly. I had failed to understand that Cindy's sister was more important to her than retiring by a certain date, and I should never have encouraged her to put money ahead of anything truly precious.

Later, when my own sister was ill, I made all kinds of "bad" financial and career choices in order to spend every minute I could with her. I assigned over half of my clients' accounts to other advisors and moved into a less impressive office. I took long breaks and spent money on airline tickets and went without a paycheck for a while, and I relied on my husband to cover the bills while I just hung out with Becky. And I frequently thought of Cindy and how smart she was. Sisters are waaaay more important than a comfortable retirement, and lucky and smart are those who discover that sooner rather than later.

Now that she is gone, I am grateful for every minute I had with my sister, and I do not care how much it may have cost, or how much longer I will have to work because I didn't concentrate on building my business at a crucial time in my career.

Now, in the course of financial planning for my clients, I understand that planning is all about getting what is truly important to them. The first question I ask every new client is: "If you were living in a perfect world, what would you do tomorrow morning, next week, next year, in 10 years?"

At first, very few of them see as clearly as Cindy did. Like "Silly Me" of long ago, they tend to think in terms of how their financial circumstances should control their lives (of course, to be fair, why else would they come to a financial planner, if not to talk money?) Invariably, I get an initial response like: "I don't think I will be able to retire until I'm 65 because that's when my pension starts."

"We can talk about the financial considerations, later," I explain. "Right now, I want to know what you *want* to be doing tomorrow morning and in the weeks and years after that. Once we know what you really want, then we will know what needs to be done with your money and with all your other resources in order to make your desires a reality."

Sure, at some point I'll be concerned about such particulars of money as investments, pension plans, income, and savings rates because I'm the mechanic who needs to get your "car" into good enough shape to make it to California and back. Money is the primary tool I work with to do my job, but it is *just one* of the many tools you need to build a good life. When it comes right down to it, everyone has other tools that can make life different and better, and most of them are far more effective than the number of dollars in any stock portfolio. This may seem cavalier, even irresponsible considering my profession, so . . .shh. . . lean in and don't tell anyone I told you this secret:

Your money is not all that important. It isn't even near the top of the list of your most important assets.

It is an asset, and as such, it can be helpful in your quest to sustain a life well lived, but large quantities of it absolutely are not necessary. Because it is the grease of our modern society, you ultimately have to have some money pass through your hands as you build your life. But never think of it as the cornerstone or the foundation of anything. If you do everything else right, the money sufficient for your life will flow to you.

At every level, money is only a part of the equation: merely a resource, not an end product. It buys the warm clothes and the food. It allows you to buy a house in a safe neighborhood, and to help your children by sending them to college. It allows you to buy some beautiful things so that your environment is pleasing. It helps you gain the goodwill of others because you can do good works with it, and it helps you transcend the ordinary life by giving you time away from working 40 hours per week so that you can go build houses and schools and treat malnourished children in an impoverished country.

Of course money can help you do all these things, and that makes it a very useful tool. But that's *all* it is. Imagine being enamored with any tool, be it a hammer or a saw or a bucket of nails. If you make more of money than that, you are, alas, letting it supersede everything that is worthwhile in your life. As Chapter 2 discussed, you begin to trek down a path that will lead you nowhere near where you really want to go. This path leads to impoverishment of the spirit, and perhaps even the pocketbook. Wealth comes more readily when you concentrate on being a productive, caring person who understands her strengths and revels in doing a certain job well.

You'll notice that this was a short chapter. Just goes to show that the role money plays in your life should mean it ain't the prima donna.

CHAPTER 4

NET WORTH VS LIFE WORTH

Poor is the man who does not know his own intrinsic worth and tends to measure everything by relative value. A man of financial wealth who values himself by his financial net worth is poorer than a poor man who values himself by his intrinsic self worth.

~Sidney Madwed (poet, business consultant)

Life Worth Assets

A financial planner must calculate her clients' Net Worth (the sum total of the dollar value of all material assets, less what is owed), just as a mechanic must check the pressure in the tires and calibrate the engine. I pay attention to Net Worth only because certain estate and income tax planning techniques are helpful at different levels of wealth. But once you have dealt with that pesky tax situation and gotten it out of the way, Net Worth is not that big a deal.

What is vastly more important is your *Life Worth*. While Net Worth is the sum total of all your stuff, your Life Worth is the sum total of what you are and what you are capable of doing. Your Life Worth assets are your knowledge and skills, your passions, your abilities, your ambitions, and your other gifts—all the various blessings you have and are.

I call these gifts "assets," because that implies a counterbalance to material "assets," i.e.: money, but they also could be called "resources." People who have lots of resources are, by definition, "resourceful;" they are able to use skills and attributes that help them to achieve things. Note there is a big difference between the meaning of "resourceful" and "wealthy," which means having lots of money. Being resourceful is what this is all about—finding ways to overcome or deal with problems that stand in the way of what you want.

Life Worth resources, or assets, make you productive: they help you better your life and the lives of others. I have listed a few Life Worth Assets below, and there are more that you may have that I haven't thought of. No one is blessed with all of these gifts. Some of us have only a few. With the basic, but very important resources that are available to you, you can build a life that can be more bountiful than you ever thought it could be. As a side note, as you increase your Life Worth by living an excellent life, focusing on positive values and results, you may find that nice, positive Net Worth number growing over the years (if you bother to notice).

Your Dreams

Dreams are like stars. . . if you follow
them they will lead you to your destiny.

~ Anonymous

Dreams are one asset everyone must have in order to live richly, and they are the most important of all the assets on your Life Worth balance sheet. By Dreams, I don't mean your fantasies of living in a mansion and wearing Vera Wang nighties on your amazing body that is always fit, even though your gorgeous boyfriend feeds you tiramisu by the pool every day. (Did I leave anything out?)

No, your Dreams are what make you *you*. They define what sustains and feeds the essential soul that is within you. Achieving the full potential of your Dreams means you fulfill a Vision for your life, and that is the purest definition of "living well."

A well defined and articulated Vision ultimately is at the core of your Life Worth, and having such a Vision will ultimately increase the value and strength of many of your other Life Worth Assets. Understanding your Vision and working to create a life in harmony with it will bring you happiness far beyond what any amount of material wealth can do. The last half of this book is devoted to helping you dream so that you can find and fulfill your Vision.

There are many other assets that you have which are critical to your Life Worth. Some of them are inborn, and some are acquired. Some you cannot increase dramatically; some can be nurtured and coaxed to grow. Of the ones that can be acquired or increased substantially with a little effort, there are four that I think are critical to your ability to significantly increase your Life Worth. These four are: Social Currency; Ambition & Drive; Knowledge, Skill, & Wisdom; and Creativity & Imagination.

Social Currency

In helping others, we shall help ourselves,
for whatever good we give out completes
the circle and comes back to us.
~Flora Edwards (industrialist, philanthropist)

As I've already described, women tend to shine when it comes to Social Currency, and while there are plenty of men who have boatloads of it, rarely do women find they are without it. Social Currency gives us the ability to relate to people, and include diplomacy, sensitivity to others, compassion, and the ability to forgive easily. A very ticklish funnybone adds to your Social Currency, as does love for and of others. Working together with plenty of goodwill and tolerance, we get more done than people working alone or in opposition to one another.

Here is a good story that illustrates how Social Currency works:

Nancy died, and due to a paperwork snafu she was sent to hell briefly. But Satan didn't like her, and she very quickly was whisked up to heaven where she belonged. Immediately, her old friends and many new ones gathered around to greet her.

"Hello Nancy! You look hungry! What would you like to eat?" asked her old friend Eleanor.

"Oh, yes I'm starving! That sweet potato casserole looks great. I'd love a bite of that," said Nancy, and Eleanor picked up a spoon and gave Nancy a big bite of it.

"Here, try some of this crawfish étouffée," interjected Sally, at the ready with a spoonful. "By the way, I hear Satan tried to snag you for awhile. What was hell like?"

"It was very strange," Nancy replied, as she scooped up some fresh green beans sautéed in truffle butter and fed it to Sally. "They all thought it was torture, even though they had the same beautiful, delicious food that we have here, and they all have the exact same gold and silver spoons to eat with that we do here."

"Really?" asked Hallie, as she gave Eleanor a big bite of gorgeous strawberry sherbet. "Why was that, I wonder? And why did they let you go so quickly?"

"Well," said Nancy, nibbling at choice morsel of fondue from Rachel's spoon, "because their spoons are longer than their arms, they think they can't eat anything, and so they're all starving. Satan hustled me out of there in a hurry when I offered the guy next to me a bite of lobster fricassee."

Women start out with the raw material for Social Currency hardwired into our brains from before day one, and we continue to grow it throughout our lives. There is a pile of evidence about the size of Mt. Rushmore that the brains of women and men are different, and that causes our thoughts, thought process, and behaviors to be different.

The differences in our brains begin occurring as early as the 8th week of gestation, when male fetuses undergo a radical change that sets them on a divergent path. As their gonads begin to develop, a surge of testosterone marinates the brain and causes—well, what else can I call it except irrevocable brain damage? [1] Poor dears.

This testosterone bath kills off some of the already-developed cells in the communication centers and causes more cells to grow in the sex and aggression centers. In girl fetuses' brains, which get no testosterone, communication centers and areas that process emotion continue merrily sprouting more cells and more robust connections.

There also is growing evidence that part of the corpus callosum, the connector cable between the left and right hemispheres, is weakened in males by the testosterone surge. Some neurophychiatrists speculate that is why men's ability to think with both the left and right hemispheres simultaneously is limited. Women tend to think with their whole brains all the time, with both hemispheres communicating back and forth with each other, while men tend to think laterally, with almost no communication between the two halves. (Your mama was right. Men *do* have a one-track mind, and here is the evidence to prove it!). Practically speaking, this causes girls to be more communicative, more emotionally competent, and more intuitive.[2]

The process of brain divergence doesn't stop at birth. Both male and female newborns undergo what is known as "infantile puberty," where babies of both sexes experience yet another wash of hormone—boys get testosterone and girls get estrogen. Endocrinologists believe these infantile estrogen surges in girls not only prompt the development of the ovaries, but also stimulate the brain circuits that enhance brain centers for observation, communication, gut feelings and nurturing tendencies.[3]

Newborn girls already have developed the brain structure and hormonal balance which affords them greater communication skills, empathy, and social sensitivity. Girls as young as one day old are more empathetic than boy babies. When exposed to the sound of others' distress, girls react more intensely than boys do. As Dr. Martin Hoffman, who specializes in pediatric developmental behavioral health observes, "Females may be more apt to imagine how it would feel if the stimuli impinging on the other were impinging on the self."[4] Girls hear and listen better,[5] read nuance in faces[6] and voice better,[7] and are much better equipped to understand the emotions and intent of others.[8]

Louann Brizendine, a Yale trained neurophychiatrist, sums up the practical results of these hormonal and brain differences in girls: "it defines our innate biological destiny, coloring the lens through which each of us views and engages the world. Typical non-testosteronized, estrogen-ruled girls are very invested in preserving harmonious relationships. From their earliest days, they live most comfortably and happily in the realm of peaceful interpersonal connections. They prefer to avoid conflict because discord puts them at odds with their urge to stay connected, to gain approval and nurture."[9]

Science has shown us that at every stage of our lives, our bodies, minds, and behaviors are deeply influenced by hormones. While estrogen plays an important function early on, the onset of puberty in girls forces a surge of other hormones, oxytocin and dopamine, both of which are further stimulated by the bonding activities of physical touch, orgasm, nursing, and emotional closeness. These hormones are pretty fantastic, natural drugs that give a rush that Dr. Brizendine describes "as intense and pleasurable as the rush that coke or heroin addicts get when they do drugs."[10] While men experience some of the pleasures of oxytocin as well, it doesn't rule them like it can rule us. No wonder we're team players!

Society and family interpersonal influences reinforce the nurturing and empathetic natures of girls. Because girls are nicer, we are expected to be nicer, and we are rewarded for it. We learn that being sweet and caring gives us more bonding pleasure—and so we live in the self-repeating cycle of nature/nurture socialization.

Working together, in a non-competitive environment, women have the capacity to make enormous progress, to get things done, and to help themselves and each other to advance. Used correctly, Social Currency can be one of the best forms of wealth that we have. There is, however, a dark side to all this: the tendency to self-sacrifice for the good of others. Many of us have been guilty of even sabotaging our own ambitions because we don't want to be too competitive with others. Any self-respecting feminist will be quick to point out that we must constantly be on guard to keep ourselves from being taken advantage of.

I agree. Girls can be sweetly stupid, especially around men who haven't quite caught on that Social Currency is supposed to be exchanged back and forth, not just grabbed and gobbled up. There has been many a time when I have gently (ok, maybe not so gently) pointed out to young women who are living with Mr. Almost Right that they are headed for financial and personal ruin because they are more concerned with making him love them than they are about finding a man who is worth loving. We must learn to be aware of the good our nurturing gifts can do without putting ourselves into a position where we sacrifice our own needs for the needs, or even desires, of others.

Social Currency works only when everyone involved is more concerned with giving than taking. The minute someone gets greedy, the "economy" begins to break down. Imagine a friend asking you for change for a ten. She is asking for a favor, because you have to dig in your purse and maybe your pockets and the floor of your car to scrape it up, but you're happy to oblige because you want to be helpful. But once you hand over the $10 in change, she says, "Thanks, I didn't tell you I would give you the ten. I just asked you to give me change for one. So long, sucker," you may not be so happy to oblige her the next time she asks for something. You could say she has blown all the Social Currency she had banked with you.

I have a client who is so sweet and dear and just a little vulnerable that I would walk through fire for her. There is something about her that makes me want to protect her, and I always take extra care to make sure things are done perfectly when she needs something. The other day, for no particular reason, she sent me flowers. She thought she was just expressing her appreciation, but what she didn't know was that I was a little blue that day—I had been working extra hard and was feeling unappreciated. Her flowers perked me up so much that the rest of my day was downright pleasurable, even though I had a pile of drudgework that I had to get through.

Now, the next time this client calls me needing something, and the same day another client who treats me like I'm just one of his disposable hired hands, no matter how hard I try to please him asks for something as well, who do you think is going to get her need taken care of first and best? Who has her pockets stuffed with Social Currency, and who's are not only empty, but full of holes?

Most of us women have learned to protect ourselves from becoming doormats. Our inborn capacity for communication and intuition can actually help us to avoid the pitfall of being too accommodating. Because we have the superior ability of interpreting "tone of voice" and body language, we have a better ability to understand people's emotions and intentions.

For instance, we immediately and effortlessly can tell when someone is being sarcastic or insincere, whereas men have more difficulty with that. The "gut instinct" we get when we know someone is deliberately trying to mislead us or intend us harm is very real.[11] We have the ability to discern when we should not trust someone and when we should refuse to be suckered by someone. Now we just have to learn to listen to that little voice that says, "Run!," pay closer attention to it, and respond, even when we're craving that oxytocin hit. I won't go into great depths with that because it is the subject of a whole other book that has already been written: Debra Condren's, *Ambition is Not a Dirty Word*. Read it sometime when you're in a really feisty mood.

While the makings for Social Currency is an innate gift, we can learn to create more of it and to use it more productively. You simply school yourself to be more aware and respectful of your own sensitivity to others and make the effort to make judgments based on the cues you so easily read. You can be more aware of the needs of others, look for ways to relate to them, help them with their problems, and seek common ground and understanding with every encounter. Learn to actively listen and to perceive the nuances of facial expressions and speech of others. Be grateful when someone does you a favor and think creatively about ways to reciprocate. Learning to see the humor in every situation, and thinking about the needs of others and how they intertwine with your own needs will make you more sensitive, more helpful, more attuned to win-win possibilities you come across every day.

As you show others your desire to nurture, you can sense the ones who respond by trusting you and who are willing to reciprocate. Just being a girl is a good start. Next, work on being a girl who deliberately goes out and panhandles and hustles for even more Social Currency.

Before I leave this subject, I have to add a postscript because I'm feeling a little guilty at the sexist tone of the discussion. (Isn't that just like a girl?) In truth, men have their strengths, too, and actually tend to be better in some things than women are. I just don't want to talk about them here. This is a book about empowering and encouraging women. Men have already written volumes about how great they are.

Ambition and Drive

If a woman is sufficiently ambitious, determined and gifted—there is practically nothing she can't do.
~Helen Lawrenson (writer)

If you know your Dreams and have determined to achieve them (that is, if you have a clear Vision. We're exploring ways to do that, beginning with the next chapter), then you already have a good bit of Ambition going for you. Ambition is simply desire, and if you have Dreams and desires, you'll have Ambition. Drive is your energy and willingness to work to fulfill the desire. That's the trickier part.

Some people are lucky in that they are born with the gift of Drive, but most of us (including myself) have to acquire it, sometimes the hard way. Ambition and Drive tend to blossom most readily when we live through some sort of dramatic event that awakens the imagination and inflames our passions. Those events could be the same ones—and probably are—that cause you to acquire and/or change your Vision. They could be as seemingly small as being told you have a special talent to as significant as losing a loved one. They might inspire you to take some action or more risk, work harder, summon up a little more grit, in order to make a change in some way.

One sure way to get a fire in your belly so that you actually get up off your duff and into action is for something awful to happen that deeply affects you. The founder of MADD, Candice Lightner, started the organization in order to get drunk drivers off the streets after she lost her 13-year-old daughter, Cari, to a drunk driver. Nancy Brinker watched her beautiful sister Susan die from breast cancer, and promised her she would help find a cure. The Susan G.

Komen foundation is now the global leader of the breast cancer eradication movement.

Candice and Nancy were ordinary people just strolling through life like we all are, until something happened to cause them to break away from their routines and do something extraordinary. Both had previously understood the dangers of drunk drivers and that breast cancer is a killer, but neither of them was driven to do anything about it until their emotions were completely engaged. Once they understood the horror of their loss, they found a new passion as a direct result of it, and their Drive revved up.

Do you have a bad habit you would like to break? Do you fail to exercise, do you overeat, do you watch too much TV? Why don't you do something about it? Because, although your mind knows you should, it's a very weak Ambition, without any Drive behind it. It's a desire without motivation. Your emotions have not been aroused enough to make you willing to do what it takes to fulfill the desire.

Oh, sure, you hate being out of shape, you feel like a sloth when you lie on the couch watching TV rather than doing something productive. But those feelings of self-loathing are not motivators! They just make you a little depressed, which makes you more apt to engage in the destructive habits. But when something really big jolts you, you may find it much easier to completely change your behavior virtually overnight.

My father smoked for his entire adult life, except for the last year of it. He tried to quit many, many times, to no avail. Sure, he knew his life would likely be shortened if he didn't quit. In his head was the knowledge that there was a real danger of cancer, and that his arteries were probably slowly being destroyed each time he puffed on one of his unfiltered Camels. But he never really understood how it would *feel* to suffer and die as a result of his bad habit.

Then he had a heart attack, and both his physical heart and his emotional heart were broken. That began a different story. As he lay in his hospital bed, weak, exhausted, feeling totally and literally not just invalid, but *in-valid*, he realized this meant he might never make love to his wife again, never be able to toss his grandchildren in the air again, indeed, never even see grandchildren yet to come. He saw the tears on his children's faces and realized that he had cheated his loved ones and himself out of years of happiness by clinging to a noisome habit.

Once he understood what it felt like to betray those who loved him and himself, he suddenly summoned the willpower he needed. He quit smoking at the moment of his heart attack, and never touched another cigarette for the rest of his much-shortened life.

During the economic downturn of 2008-2011, some of my clients lost their high-paying, prestigious positions with companies they had worked with for decades. At first, they were stunned with grief upon hearing of their layoffs, but then they eventually came to understand that they now had a great opportunity to break free of their golden handcuffs and do what they had secretly been yearning to do for years. Now some of them are feeling like they are finally doing what they really should have been doing all along—pursuing the careers they had dreamed about. Until they lost their jobs, they had been too comfortable and complacent to make the break.

Sometimes it takes a heart attack, the senseless death of a child, a spouse walking out the door, a friend dying as a result of drinking and driving, or some major catastrophe to make people actually understand with their emotional hearts what their bad habits or bad actions or bad situations actually mean. A single, precipitous event can change behavior and a life far more than simply the half-hearted fancy you may have about doing something important.

It isn't always something bad that happens that can jolt you out of your ordinary life and into something bigger and more wonderful. Queen Elizabeth I became one of the greatest monarchs the world has ever known, but she wouldn't have been in the position to be that if she had not been the last surviving legitimate child of Henry VIII.

Other lucky moments can change a life for good. A schoolteacher from Taiwan won tens of millions of dollars in a 2005 lottery and gave every penny of it to help disadvantaged children, and a Canadian couple recently did something similar with their lottery winnings. One of my clients set up a self-perpetuating foundation for refugee relief after receiving a sizeable inheritance.

While it's debatable that it was a wonderful thing for shy, awkward Diana Spencer to stumble into the view of Prince Charles and became the Princess of Wales, there is no doubt that her being catapulted into that role was the thing that made her such a successful and beloved icon of goodwill and philanthropy. If she had not become the Princess, she would not have been able to accomplish what she did. Because of her, organizations like Centerpoint, a group that aids homeless youth, the Leprosy Mission, various cancer and AIDS charities, and the International Red Cross have been able to reach and help more people. She was highly influential in the battle to remove sleeping land mines and helped to provide funds for those injured by them.

Of course, I'm not advocating that we all sit around and wait for something really big to happen to us so that we will get busy and turn ourselves into energized, motivated people, raring to do good things. If we wait around to be discovered or to marry Prince Awful Charming or win millions of dollars, the chances are pretty good that we will never do anything at all.

But if we push ourselves to understand what could happen if we don't change things or what we could accomplish if we set our minds to it, we are less likely to need a lightning bolt to jolt Ambition and Drive into us. There are other ways to light the fire of Ambition, to break the bonds of inertia, to look up from our complacent existence so that we see what is possible and be inspired to achieve something more.

The first, and most effective way to summon up the energy it takes to make a change is to exercise our Imagination (see the next section). If our Imagination can be ignited in the same way it is whenever we get a big shock, we can begin to see and feel the consequences of our actions and inactions and understand how important it is to do something about it. The Imagination is like a muscle in that it must be exercised in order to grow strong. Taking your Dreams seriously is the best way to bulk up a puny Imagination. Find your Vision, which is the spark, the passion that flames up when you give yourself permission to dream without fear.

Another way to help you increase your Ambition and Drive is simply to be encouraged by yourself and by others. As a matter of fact, the reason I decided to write this book is that daily, I see firsthand how just a little encouragement helps people grow the confidence to step up and do things that they may never have done without that little nudge.

Few people believe in themselves unless someone else believes in them too, but it's sad the way we fail to let others see how much confidence we have in them, even though it is very easy, almost effortless to do. It's far easier for others to see your possibilities and to minimize your limitations, because they don't fear for you the way you fear for yourself. They don't see your shortcomings the way you do. They just see the simple fact of you: your skills, your personality, your Life Worth Assets. They don't care about your insecurities, and even if they do see them, they are less likely to give them undue importance. They have a better perspective of the forest because they aren't one of the trees.

If someone tells me she wants to take a year off from her current job and go live abroad, I can see how that is possible, even easily accomplished. I can see that she has the financial wherewithal to live without an income for a year or more, that she has marketable skills and the capability of getting another job when she returns home. I see her strengths, how hard she works, and how dedicated she is to excellence, and I can even see her having the ability to earn an income, if necessary, while living in another country. It's easy for me to see the way her face lights up when she thinks of being in a different culture, which tells me she could benefit from the break and that her life will be better for the experience.

Sure, it's easy for me to see all this about someone else. But when people are at a critical crossroad where they either have to act or not, to be brave or cowardly, they tend to immediately see the "impossibilities" or the scary "whatifs:" What if they can't replace their old job when they get back? What if they hate being away? What if they run out of money while they are gone, or have to use up their retirement funds? What will happen to their house while they are gone?

They talk themselves out of making this big step because they start envisioning all the bad things that can happen before they even give their Dreams full consideration. It's human nature, and also very prudent, to examine the possible bad outcomes of any venture you are contemplating. Such wariness is healthy in that it keeps us from doing stupid things like hitting the tequila and taking a road trip to Las Vegas, picking up a hot hunk at the casino, and staggering off with him to the Elvis-inspired Chapel of Wedded Love. It also forces us to understand and critically examine what bad things could happen so that we can take steps to mitigate or circumvent those unfortunate possibilities.

But the scary "whatifs" also can undermine our self-confidence and sabotage our ability to act, when we allow them to grow out of control. That is why we need encouragers, people who tell us when we're being silly with our fears, friends who will push us and tell us that we are capable of doing extraordinary things and becoming extraordinary people. They will hold us to the promises we make to ourselves and remind us of our strengths when we forget them. Assign at least one of your friends the role of mentor who can push you to not only believe in yourself, but also hold you to your promises to live the way you really want. Start a support group of people who will encourage each other's dreams. Get other drivers to help your Drive.

This idea of surrounding yourself with encouraging people to help you improve your life is not new. You probably have heard many times that positive people are good for you and negative people are toxic, and that you need to cultivate as many positive-thinking friends as you can. Moreover, according to the conventional wisdom, you should run as fast as you can from anyone who might drag you down with her negative attitude.

Frankly, that harsh philosophy always bothered me. You know as well as I do that it's mean to dump a friend who is hurting, and anyone who is consistently negative is usually hurting in some way. How right is it to turn your back on a friend when she most needs you? Wouldn't this be selfish and compromise your own integrity?

Deborah Griffitts Hining

Yes, we should try our best to cultivate new friends who have positive attitudes, but that does not mean we necessarily need to ditch our old friends (if they truly are friends). Rather than expect to suck all the goodness up that others have to offer, and ignore the ones who have little to give, take it upon yourself to give some goodness to others. Make a concentrated effort to be an encourager. There are too few of us out there. All Dreams need encouragement, and people who have a lot of negative thoughts need it more than anyone.

By encouraging others, you will not only help them, but you will build your Social Currency, and you will learn how to deal with negative energy. As you find ways of stopping others from throwing up barriers, starting up the "yes-buts," you will be able to catch yourself in the act of sabotaging your own Dreams, and you will learn how to overcome your own negative thoughts and fears. (More on this in Chapter 9)

This does not mean that you should hang on to people who claim to be your friends but who, in reality, are *not*. Sometimes the worst enemies of your Dreams are those who say they have your best interests at heart. It's ok to spend time and energy encouraging others who need help reaching their own Dreams, but have fears they need to deal with. Their scary "whatifs" are directed toward their own hopes, not yours. But when people start trying to tell you that you are likely to fail, and you get the feeling they *want* you to fail for some reason, it's time to say goodbye. Don't waste your Social Currency or your goodwill on them. Their empty hands are out, poised to grab, and they have no desire for a reciprocating relationship.

I once had a beautiful, bright, talented, ultra sophisticated student who also happened to have recently held the title of Miss Black America. She wanted to pursue a singing career, but she confided in me that she wasn't sure that she was good enough to get a contract with a record company, even though one had already expressed an interest in her. She was delaying getting back in touch because her "best friend" had, with great compassion, expressed some doubts about her ability to make it in the competitive music industry. She had warned her that she probably would be happier if she stayed home, got married, and pursued some less grand vision.

My student should have buffed up her innate ability to discern when someone is being insincere or deliberately hurtful. The last time I talked to her, she was sitting in a stew of her own self-doubts, too insecure about her talent (which everyone else saw as enormous) to begin the process of launching her career. Her "friend" had stolen her possibilities by deliberately singeing the wings of her Dreams. Those are the naysayers you need to run from.

Imagination and Creativity

Lack of money is no obstacle.
Lack of an idea is an obstacle.

~Ken Hakuta (inventor)

I've already discussed Imagination within the context of Dreams and Ambitions because all these gifts rely on each other and reinforce the others. The more you have of one Life Worth Asset, the easier it is to make the others more accessible and valuable. Imagination gives you understanding of things not yet seen or felt, and helps you envision the consequences of certain actions and inactions. Creativity allows you to find new ways to solve problems and to make things happen in unexpected and unconventional ways.

While some people are born with full-blown Imaginations & Creativity, these assets actually can be grown within a mind that's about as pedestrian as a toadstool. Believe it or not, Walt Disney was fired from his first job at the Kansas City Star newspaper because he lacked creativity![12] Obviously, he later became much more creative because he worked to cultivate it. We'll delve into this more fully in Chapter 9, because it is essential that you have creative tools at your disposal as you create your life.

Knowledge, Skill, & Wisdom

Through wisdom is a house built; and by understanding it is established; and by knowledge shall every room be filled with precious and pleasant riches.

~Proverbs 24:3

The more Knowledge you have, the more able you are to tap into your resourcefulness, and the better equipped you will be to do what you want to do. Knowledge is entirely an acquired asset, totally unlike high intelligence or talent, so try to never stop learning. It's nice that gaining Knowledge is pretty easy these days. There's a community college on virtually every corner. Night classes are more fun and interesting than reality TV, and the library is free.

One of the areas in which women tend to be painfully ignorant is the realm of money and investing. Because I frequently see the disasters people can create because they have made poor decisions due to a lack of knowledge about their money, I want everyone to understand how important this is. According to a 2005 study by Merrill Lynch, 47% of women, (vs. 30% of men) feel that their knowledge of investing is inadequate. In truth, their perception of what they know may actually be inflated.[13] According to a 2008 survey by Peter Tufano, a professor of financial management at the Harvard Business School, and Annamaria Lusardi, an economics professor at Dartmouth College, two thirds of Americans did not understand the most basic principle of how compound interest works.[14]

Over half the respondents in a Princeton University survey said that they had learned "not too much" or "nothing at all" about financial issues at school.[15] When I ask a new client if she knows how our graduated tax system works, I get a blank look about 99% of the time.

Not understanding the basics about money management can be devastating to a modern woman, and you certainly owe it to yourself to become financially literate. Not to do so is as irresponsible as getting behind the wheel of a car without first learning how to drive; it's pretty much guaranteed that somebody (namely you) is going to get hurt. According to Niall Ferguson in *The Ascent of Money*:

[Understanding] finance . . . exaggerates the differences between us, enriching the lucky and the smart, impoverishing the unlucky and not-so smart. . . .The more integrated the world's financial markets become, the greater the opportunities for financially knowledgeable people wherever they live—and the bigger the risk of downward mobility for the financially illiterate. . . The rewards for 'getting it' have never been so immense. And the penalties for financial ignorance have never been so stiff.[16]

Although I have been yammering on about how money itself is not your most important resource, I do want to make it clear that understanding and Knowledge about how money works, no matter how much or little you have, is *vital*. You need to know how to take care of your tools properly, and the ability to manage money is a Life Worth Asset that no one should be without. While this book does not directly speak to helping you learn more about money management, I encourage you to find one that does, or find a good financial advisor to guide you, so that you can know how to use the money you do have to its fullest potential.

Similar to your Knowledge is your Skills and practical abilities that make you more useful to yourself and to others. Want to learn to tango? To crochet? To hang wallpaper? To speak Farsi? Great! Do it, and you've just increased your Life Worth. Keep doing it more and more, and the chances are very good that you will also increase your Net Worth as a result.

Wisdom is simply understanding how to put Knowledge to use for the best advantage. It allows you to make good decisions because you understand the full consequences of actions. As you go through the exercises in the following chapters, you will find your Wisdom increasing.

It's pretty obvious how to increase your Knowledge & Skill, but in order to increase those, you may need to first increase your Ambition & Drive, Imagination & Creativity, and Curiosity. You know you need to do research or go back to school or learn a new skill in order to do all the things you want to do, but if you don't have any Curiosity or the Drive to do what you may need, you'll never take that first class. You'll find excuses to keep you from doing what needs to be done to increase your Knowledge. The funny thing is, increasing your Knowledge & Skill will automatically increase your Curiosity, Imagination & Creativity, and your Ambition & Drive. All your Life Worth Assets compliment and build the others.

As I have said, all the above are very important Life Worth Assets which can be cultivated. When you build them, you will find them reinforcing all your other Life Worth Assets. What follows is a brief list of other Assets that could be very helpful to you. Some can be reinforced and expanded; some are merely innate, and they are difficult to increase. These include, but are not limited to:

Curiosity

If you tell me that curiosity killed the cat,
I say only the cat died nobly.
~Arnold Edinborough (writer, historian)

Unless you have Curiosity, you'll never want to learn new things. A curious mind leads you to explore and inclines you to seek out new ways of thinking and of doing things. It leads you to become smarter and more interesting, too. The best way to increase Curiosity is to increase your Knowledge. The more you learn, the more you want to know more.

Intelligence, Talents, and Other Inherent Gifts

Deborah Griffitts Hining

We are all gifted for something
~Marie Curie
(physicist, twice winner of the Nobel Prize)

Exceptional gifts such as musical or athletic talent, great beauty, or a photographic memory are not as easily acquired as some of the other Life Worth Assets, but you can, indeed, increase your inherent gifts with lots of hard work. Granted, most of us aren't going to turn ourselves into a Maria Callas or a Meryl Streep by sheer force of will and hard work, but we can come close if we are motivated enough. Thank goodness, most of us have at least one or two inherent gifts to start out with. And if we feel we have missed out in some areas, and we don't want to put the effort into changing our basic intellect or level of talent, we can make up for what we lack in other ways, with other gifts and other Assets. Helen Keller graduated from college and became an internationally influential author, lecturer, and political activist, despite the fact that she was both blind and deaf from early childhood.

Flexibility

The main thing is not to know how you'll succeed.
It is to know what you'll do if your idea fails.
~Arthur Bejack

Things almost never turn out the way you imagine they will. No matter how much you plan, something is going to pop up to get in your way, or something more wonderful than what you had planned for will present itself. Flexibility both allows you to be open to serendipity and allows you to adapt and find alternate resources and strategies when the ones you thought you could rely on prove inadequate. Creativity helps increase your ability to be flexible.

Expect that your Vision for yourself will evolve over time because you will fulfill one Vision and move on to another, or your circumstances may change dramatically. Occasionally we all have to reinvent ourselves, so be open to moving on when new situations cause you to change your worldview. Marriage, children, an empty nest, widowhood, divorce, the loss or change of a job or career, an unexpected large inheritance, a religious epiphany, a jail term, all of these would thrust upon you a new reality which might cause you to change the way you view yourself and your world. So resolve to be flexible, and frequently revisit your Vision to make sure it is always right for you.

Courage and Leadership

Some leaders are born women
~Unknown, but obviously someone very wise!

Courageous leadership gives you the ability to face adversity in order to right a wrong or to persevere under hardship, and the ability to ascertain a problem, see its solution, and lead others to effect change. Leaders have self-control, discipline, modesty, perseverance, and the ability to make thoughtful decisions. It takes courage and tenacity to get over the obstacles that continually pop up while you are striving to live well.

Deborah Griffitts Hining

Spirituality

If ye have faith as a grain of mustard seed,
ye shall say unto this mountain, "Remove
hence to yonder place," and it shall re-
move.

~Jesus, *Matthew 17:20*

Connection to the spiritual realm helps you to seek a
larger good and to appreciate the mysteries of the universe
and be grateful for them. Hope, faith, and prayer can take
you a long way because they give you additional confidence
and empowerment. A part of this gift is manifested in Grace,
the ability to see the beauty or humor or goodness in people,
things and situations.

Time

With time and patience the mulberry
leaf becomes a silk gown.

~ Chinese Proverb

The more Time you have to accomplish something,
the more likely you are to be able to make it happen. We're
used to expecting instant gratification, but good things take
Time to bloom. (As you may have heard, Rome wasn't built
in a day.) To be rich in Time is a fantastic blessing. If you
have plenty and are wise enough not to squander it, there's
no telling what you can accomplish.

You can make more Time for yourself by protecting
your health and energies, and you can also borrow it from
somewhere else. Rather than wasting Time on inane activities
such as watching TV or hanging out in the pool hall, you
can use it productively to build the life you want.

You can also use other people's Time. By working together with others, you can let the same Time be used to fulfill the needs of many. As an example, suppose you and your neighbor take turns cooking dinner. Tonight you make a meal for two families and free her up to take the landscaping course she wants take. Tomorrow night, she can cook for you so you can attend your dance class. Use your Social Currency (a renewable resource) to purchase yourself some extra Time.

There are times when it makes sense to buy other people's Time. If you don't know what you are doing when it comes to some important tasks, you'll end up wasting Time (and money) by futzing around trying to do things you are not qualified to do and don't really enjoy doing. I don't cut my own hair or sew my own clothes or change the oil in my car. Don't try to be such a do-it-yourselfer that you waste precious Time trying to do things you don't really like doing. If you feel you can't financially afford to hire professional help, you can always find a way to barter with skills you are good at.

Health and Energy

It is health that is real wealth
and not pieces of gold and silver.
~ Mahatma Gandhi

Oh, to be perpetually blessed with these gifts! When Health and Energy are with us, we are never completely aware of their value. When they leave us, we find that we have lost the very best of friends. Cherish and preserve your Health and Energy in every way you can. They enhance your other Life Worth assets exponentially.

Poverty

The greatest man in history was the poorest
~Ralph Waldo Emerson

Bet you didn't expect this one, did you? But think about all the people who are enormously successful who grew up very poor. If you have lived in poverty, you have not had the distractions and "addictions" you would have had if you were born affluent. People who have the gift of Poverty feel free to take risks for what is truly important because they have nothing to lose if they fail. They are grateful for what they have, and they rarely lose perspective about what they deserve and what gives them joy. Dolly Parton, Oprah Winfrey, and J.K. Rowling are just a few who have risen far above the Poverty in which they have lived, and they all have not only made significant contributions to the world, but they have been happy with the lives they made for themselves.

A different kind of Poverty can be given to you in the same way Ambition is given to you when it is caused by a painful, precipitous event. If you lose something very precious to you, such as a loved one or your Health, you may feel you have nothing else of importance to lose if you go out on a limb. The rewards become much more important than the risk.

Money

Money is the root of all evil, and yet it is such
a useful root that we cannot get on without it
any more than we can without potatoes
~Louisa May Alcott

Sure, you need to consider Material Wealth an Asset on your Life Worth balance sheet. It is a pretty good tool if you use it properly. If you have a lot of this, along with good doses of other assets above, you might be able to get a little more accomplished a little faster, if you know how to use it. As I've been yelling at the top of my lungs, the ability to use Money wisely is a far better asset than the Money itself.

Power

Women have to harness their power—it's absolutely true. It's just learning not to take the first no. And if you can't go straight ahead, you go around the corner.

~Cher

Women tend to shy away from wanting/using Power, and as a result, it is one tool we often hobble along without. Power is the ability to control things and people to use them to your advantage. Most women prefer to have Power only over their own lives, but that's really all you need. If you are able to direct your own life, you'll have much greater satisfaction with the life you can make for yourself. One area you can have Power over in your life is Money, but in order to do that, you may need to increase your Knowledge.

Life Worth Assets at Work

Anything is possible, given the correct and creative use of your assets. If you really want to go to school, take a trip, start a business, alleviate the suffering of children in your city, free Tibet, or just about anything else, you actually can do it, even if you don't have a penny saved up. It just takes you being determined and resourceful enough in other ways.

Here's a quick example, although we will be looking in depth at how you can use your Life Worth Assets in later chapters: Let's say you want a garden in your back yard. If you had lots of Money but little in the way of other Life Worth Assets, you could simply hire someone to make it for you. You would end up with a garden, probably even a very beautiful one, but you probably wouldn't think of it as a notable accomplishment. It would be there merely for your viewing pleasure.

But let's say you have no Money at all. Now this is where your other Life Worth Assets come into play. If you really want a garden and will be happy working in it, you can make one without Money, using just your own Time, Creativity, Energy, a borrowed shovel, and your ability to talk your friends into helping. You might need to increase your Knowledge and Skill, but if you have enough Ambition, or desire for the garden, you will be able to increase and use those Assets enough to complete tasks.

You would go online or to the library to discover what plants grow best under what conditions. You could use your Social Currency, asking others to share their Knowledge with you, and you might also ask them for cuttings from their gardens.

Once you knew what to look for, you could dig up wild native plants growing in ditches. You could ask a farmer if you could have some of his rotting cow manure and begin composting your own table scraps. In short, you would use a certain set of skills and specific resources you already have in abundance, or which you could acquire, to make the garden.

This approach might seem to be more cumbersome, but how much more proud would you be of yourself and your garden if you did it this way? How much more pleasure will it give you?

And here is something else to consider: unless it is given to you without you having earned it, Money is merely the product of the use of your other Life Worth Assets. You use your Knowledge, Skills, Strength, Leadership, and so forth to earn Money. Think of how much Time and Energy you would have to put in working at your job in order to make enough to pay someone to create the garden. I think it would improve the quality of your life more to use that Time planning, digging and planting rather than logging hours at the office.

And besides, you'll sure save a lot in taxes! Every time money changes hands, Uncle Sam and his offspring stick their hands in there to grab some. Let's say your employer has about $1000 to spend for you to work a little extra to complete a certain job. She will use every penny of it, but not every penny she has for the job will go to you. She also has to pay your unemployment tax and half your Social Security tax. For your part, you will pay the other half of your Social Security tax and all of your federal and state income tax. When you buy plants at the nursery, you will have to cough up the extra sales tax. So while your employer started out with $1000 to pay for your Time, Skill, and labor, you end up with only with enough to purchase a garden worth as little as half that much, depending on the state you live in and your income tax bracket.

Deborah Griffitts Hining

As you read farther, you will understand the value of your Life Worth Assets and how to put them to their best use. You're about to discover how wealthy you really are!

CHAPTER 5

A QUEEN NEEDS A QUEENDOM

Linus, do you know what I intend? I intend to be a queen. When I grow up I'm going to be the biggest queen there ever was and I'll live in this big palace with a big front lawn and have lots of beautiful dresses to wear and when I go out in my coach all the people will wave and I will shout at them! And in the summertime I will go to my summer palace and I'll wear my crown in swimming and everything, and all the people will cheer and I will shout at them. . . . Nobody should be kept from being a queen if she wants to be one!

~Lucy Van Pelt, from
You're a Good Man Charlie Brown
by Charles Schultz

There is an old Ben Franklin ditty that I learned in elementary school that is supposed illustrate the very true fact that you must take care of small details so that big things can be accomplished. It goes like this:

For want of the nail, the shoe was lost.
For want of the shoe, the horse was lost.
For want of the horse, the rider was lost.
For want of the rider, the battle was lost.
For want of the battle, the kingdom was lost.

That makes sense. You'd better mind your horse's shoes before you go into battle. If your horse isn't securely shod, you could have trouble, perhaps even miss an important opportunity to win the day. A loose horseshoe could ultimately make the difference between keeping the kingdom safe and losing it to the marauding hoards.

This is a great lesson, but let's look at it in more than one way. Not only do we need to take care of the small things that need to be done, we also need to keep our eyes on the larger things as well. Our paradigm changes if we think of it from the top down—or from the bottom up.

What if there were no kingdom—or rather, in our case Queendom? What if there were no gleaming citadel on the hill, no fertile farmlands, no beautiful lakes and valleys and villages, no people that we treasure so much it would be worth riding into battle and risking our lives for?

How impoverished would we be if there was nothing important enough to make us willing to face dangers, that all we cared about was how well our horses are shod? Or how well *we* are shod, for that matter. Having a closet full of Prada shoes might be a nice thing, but who thinks it is the most important thing? Nobody but Imelda Marcos, I hope, and even she came to realize that line of thinking was flawed.

> Imelda Marcos and her husband, Ferdinand, ruled the Philippines from the 1930s until the 80s. In 1983, the citizens, angry at their extravagance and cruelty, revolted, forcing Imelda and Ferdinand to flee. Imelda left behind 2,700 pairs of shoes in a closet in just *one* of her homes. Here is a case where, for love of the shoes the Queendom was lost. You have to wonder how many purses she had.

Battles and wars are a big deal. Even skirmishes where people could be killed or injured are big deals. Why on earth would we risk life and limb to go into battle? Indeed, why would it matter if we kept our horses well shod or not, if it ultimately didn't mean keeping or losing something very precious?

Your Vision Quest

Nothing happens unless first a dream
~Carl Sandburg

The difference between people who live well and those who don't essentially boils down to how committed they are to their very own Queendom (or kingdom) that they treasure above all else. People who live well have a firm grasp of what is important to them. One of the hallmarks of living well is *knowing* that you are living well, knowing you are happy with who you are and what you have.

Living well means you have thought about and developed a firm Vision about what you really, truly want from life, and from that Vision, you have built a life that you know is right for you. Vision gives you the passion to do what it takes, even if it means battling unfavorable circumstances or fierce enemies, to build the reality that you want.

While most people have some glimmers of their Vision—they sort of kind of know what they maybe would like their lives to look like, most have not thought carefully enough to truly envision and articulate it clearly.

In fact, most people never even think about it at all. The very idea of looking for a Life Vision seems bizarre, or at the very least, self-indulgent. After all, claiming the right to your very own Queendom *does* seem a bit narcissistic, doesn't it? For various reasons, people rarely actively plan a way to make their lives better or richer or more meaningful. Most of us just stroll—or struggle—along from one set of circumstances to the next, and let whatever events that unfold create our reality. We make decisions based on what's easiest or what makes sense or feels right at the time, and we justify our lack of purpose by saying we just "take life as it comes."

By accepting whatever pops up in our paths without deliberating whether it is worthwhile, we allow circumstances to set us on a trajectory that may eventually be very difficult to change. Then we just get used to the way things are, or what we think they should be, or what our immediate circle of friends and relatives or Madison Avenue tell us they should be that we never plumb the depths of who we really are and what we really should be doing. We never fully appreciate the magnitude of what is possible for us because we don't even realize there is a possibility other than what we see directly in front of us.

Our good old American work ethic and our constant need to be "busy" causes us to get up every morning and pick up the plow, and we work at the mundane business of life almost every minute of every day. As we plow, we look ahead only far enough to see the next rock that might wreck our blades. Rarely do we look at the end of the row. Even more rarely do we think about how beautiful the garden we are working in is going to be as a result of all this work.

Every day we plow in the same furrows, and we keep reinforcing and deepening the same old ruts every time we pass back over the rows we plowed before. Before long, whenever we look out to the future, we see only the same ruts, and eventually, we lose the ability to see anything else, to even think, to be creative, or to see other possibilities. We're so busy looking just a few feet in front of our plows that we almost never look up at the sky.

Maybe we don't even really know why we are plowing. Somebody just put a plow in our hands and slapped the mule's rump, and off we went. We may not like it, but we don't know what else to do, and besides, it's a lot of trouble to jump a row and take off across the field to plow against the grain.

Possibilities abound around us, but finding those possibilities requires that we take our eyes off our immediate tasks of plowing: completing that report, changing the diaper, cooking dinner, checking email, whatever it is that sucks the minutes out of our day so fast that it vanishes without our having been aware that we are living in it.

And it isn't all work that we're doing: much is just fruitless activity—playing computer games or watching TV. Then, somehow, the day is done, and so is the night, and now it's time to get up and get behind the plow again. Sometimes we wonder, "Where did it go?" and maybe we mourn its loss, but we don't know how to slow down the evaporation of days. We may feel a vague uneasiness that life seems to be outside our control, but most of us push that feeling aside and go back to plowing.

I have heard some people say this is the way it is supposed to be. They feel uneasy at the idea of "planning" life. Philosophically, we have been taught during the last century to "live in the moment," and not let the future or the past invade our experience of this particular, precious moment. Some fear that deliberately planning for the future can take away spontaneity and make us become too involved with what might be rather than what really is, so that we sacrifice the present.

Yes, of course we should enjoy the worth of each moment, and we should not let regrets from the past or expectations of the future cloud our ability to experience life as we live in it. But when we just mindlessly plow, we really aren't living in the moment. In fact, we aren't really living at all. We're just doing that mind-numbing work or activity

Deborah Griffitts Hining

that gets us through the day. And by not making deliberate choices to direct our future, we sacrifice precious time, squandering what is available to create the next moment.

It's ok to plow. As a matter of fact, we have to in order to create a beautiful garden. But we should never plow mindlessly, stuck in ruts that give us no vision, and no options. We should battle the tendency to allow the daily tasks of living interfere with our larger need to discover and nurture our Visions. We need to deliberately plow for the Queendom we have chosen and built for ourselves, and not waste time plowing a garden we don't cherish, growing the wrong crops, failing to work thoughtfully for the life we were meant to live.

Know Thyself

~The Greek Philosophers

What is your Vision? How do you define your Queendom? Most people discover that their Life's Vision is pretty simple. They want to live good, honest lives. They want to be connected to others in some way that benefits those others as well as themselves. They want to work at something meaningful and enjoyable. Appreciating the bounties of life, finding a soul mate and raising happy, healthy, well adjusted children, making a contribution in some way is a common Vision of many.

Some special people are made to fulfill larger Visions and connect directly to larger communities. Rosa Parks, Lottie Moon, Florence Nightingale, for example, were brave souls who reached for more, and were willing to give up much in the way of creature comforts and safety in order to fulfill the larger role that destiny had planned for them.

Most people, including myself, aren't that ambitious. It doesn't matter if your Vision is smallish in the grand scheme of things. All that is important, at least for now, is that you are able to honestly and clearly identify and articulate what is important to YOU. That is more than most people do in a lifetime.

Finding your unique Vision can be a struggle because you may have to fight a tendency to remain locked in your current circumstances and the repetitive patterns of the life you've gotten used to. As bestselling author Leo F. Buscaglia, says, "The hardest battle you're ever going to fight is the battle to be just you." But once you decide to find your Vision, it shouldn't be terribly hard. All you have to do is *know yourself*, which means no more than knowing what you like and what you want. To really know your own desires is to understand your Vision.

If you read Chapter 2, you understand that sometimes, what we think we want is not really what we want. We are so much a product of our environments that many times we "want" things that can actually make us miserable, or at least sidetrack us from seeking what we *really* want. We get so busy loving those empty, glittery bags we've snatched up that we lose sight of what is important to us, and consequently it is difficult to clearly see our own Queendom—the one we would live in if we concentrated all our resources on building what we see in our best Life Visions.

To discover what it means for you to live well, you have to spend some time in conversation with yourself. Defining your Vision for your Queendom could take a short time if you've already been thinking about it, or if you were born with a certain gift that drives your life almost outside your control. I doubt that Wonder Woman or Venus Williams spent much time agonizing over what they should do with their lives. Most likely your Vision will take longer to develop. It will also change and evolve over time as your situation and experiences change.

What follows is a process I have been developing for many years to help people understand what they really want in life so that they can begin to live more deliberately and be in greater control of their circumstances. If you take the trouble to follow this process, you will accomplish some amazing things. So let's get busy and start designing and building your very own Queendom!

CHAPTER 6

RIDERS, PREPARE!

Boot, saddle, to horse, away!
~Robert Browning

If your Queendom is a life that fits into your well thought-out Vision, the life best suited for you, you need good Riders, warriors who will lead the battle to keep that Queendom safe. Riders take care of and manage the horses, making sure they are fed and well shod. As the higher thinking beings in any cavalry, they have an overview: they know what larger accomplishments must be met, and they are able to direct specific actions to make the battle successful.

As you build your Queendom, your Riders *are* the overview, the specific Goals you develop that organize and drive everything else. They give you guidance so that you can carry through with the appropriate actions and thought that will build and protect your Queendom.

Your Desires Define You

The first principle of success is desire - knowing what you want. Desire is the planting of your seed.
~Robert Collier (author, *The Secret of the Ages*)

I once had a friend named Michael who was an architect but who thought like an engineer. He was analytical to the bone. He loved details. He never did anything without doing extensive research first, ferreting out every possible pro and con. This man spent more time planning than doing.

When it was time to buy a new car, he did his research, carefully weighing cost, gas mileage, maintenance histories, cost of replacement parts, and dependability. He finally decided that he should buy a gently used Honda Accord, so off to the dealership he went, checkbook in hand.

While at the dealership, a cherry red Camero caught his eye, and in a weak moment, he test-drove it. This flashy car woke up another part of him, and he found he really enjoyed the power, the speed, and the sense of freedom he found in it. After the test drive was over, he reluctantly surrendered the keys and went back to the task at hand of buying a Honda Accord. He went home with a nearly new, gray one that was less likely to show dirt. Naturally, he didn't want to drive around in a dirty looking car.

To his surprise, he dreamed about the cherry red Camero that night, and the next day he found himself researching Cameros in an idle moment. The stats didn't please him. This was not a practical car. High maintenance, a gas hog, high insurance premiums, more likely to get stopped for speeding. This was not the kind of car he needed. He was satisfied with his Honda.

But that night, he dreamed about the cherry red Camero again, only this time, he dreamed it was a convertible. The next day, and for several days and weeks thereafter, he found he couldn't stop thinking about it. But every time the vision of himself zooming along the highway in it popped into his head, he pushed it aside, telling himself that he would never be so foolish as to buy that car.

Six months later, he traded in his gently used, gray Honda Accord for a brand new, cherry red Camero Z28 convertible, with a 6.2-liter V8 engine. It had 450 horses under the hood and got a whopping 18 mpg on the highway. He was thrilled with it.

After Michael bought his new Camero, he didn't become less analytical, but he noticed a side of himself he hadn't paid much attention to before. He found himself loosening up in many ways. He had been looking for the "right" woman for a long time, and, as expected, had a list of specifications.

In order not to waste time on a first date with women who would not likely fit his criteria, he always had done background checks on girls he considered dating to make sure they were suitable before he asked them out. They needed to be compatible with him: analytical, serious, no-nonsensical. Until this point, none of the women he dated really thrilled him. He was single at 32, and still looking. But after he bought his Camero, his freewheeling, bleached blonde, actress neighbor asked him for a ride in it, and they were married within the year.

When I saw them sometime later, she confided in me: "I never would have considered dating someone like Michael. He seemed so uptight at first, but I couldn't be happier that we found each other. You wouldn't believe how thrilled I am with my little nerdy husband," she said, as she slipped her hand into his and looked at him with longing. He, obviously, was just as smitten.

So what had happened to my uptight, analytical friend? He discovered he had a desire that he thought was inconsistent with what he should be wanting. For years he willed himself to do what he thought he should do, ignoring the little voice that popped up occasionally, saying "I'd really like. . ." But ultimately, that desire proved more powerful than his will. It became the driving force behind his thoughts, and ultimately, his actions.

Michael was lucky. After he bent just a little and allowed room for some of his suppressed desires to emerge, his life changed. He discovered the real person and the real needs underneath the one-dimensional character he had groomed himself to be. Once he allowed his Dreams to rise to the surface, he was able to embrace all of who and what he was. He is no less analytical than before—he still drives his wife crazy with his meticulous ways, but his passionate and impulsive side keeps them both happy.

You have desires that may be suppressed, as well, because you may think they are unreasonable or silly or un-attainable. But there is a way of living that suits you, and if you honor your Dreams and desires, that life will fully flower, and your Queendom will fit you as perfectly as those 50% spandex jeans that you practically live in. Let's begin the process of mapping out your Queendom by figuring out what it is you really want.

Step 1: Embrace Your Dreams

Necessary Tools:
 Thinking cap, classical music recordings, lined notebook paper, pen, copier, scissors, paper clips, pretty bowl, some quiet time to yourself

To find your Vision, begin understanding what you want, including the secret things. Then make your Dreams concrete by expressing them as specific Goals. Get over any ideas that "desires" are bad because they are overly self-in-dulgent, or that "Goals" should be weighty or achievable, or even reasonable. Don't even think about whether or not you can afford any of the things you want to do. Be indulgent with yourself, just as you would be indulgent with a loved one who told you about something she secretly longed to do.

Let's start by putting on some classical music, which will help you be more creative. Pick up a piece of lined note-book paper. Uh-oh, this is starting to sound like work, and it's usually the place in self-help books that I skip over. And

I bet you are balking right now because you know you're going to have to make a list—and who wants to make a list?

Well, you make lists all the time because you know they help. You write grocery lists and guest lists. You make a list of all the things that must get done when you start work in the morning. You make a household chore list on Saturday morning: "do the laundry, mop the kitchen, take the cat to the vet." But these lists that you write every day are those that merely facilitate your plowing.

Now you need to write a list that is going to facilitate your Vision. This is a moment to stop plowing and begin to look at the sky, the possibilities, the hopes for your Queendom. And it works. By putting this in writing, you will articulate and elevate your desires; you will realize that they are worthy of becoming the building blocks of a life well lived.

Besides, there is a practical reason to put things in writing. The human mind is able to retain only about 5-9 chunks of information at a time. After 12 seconds, recall is poor, and after 20 seconds, information disappears altogether. If you don't write your ideas down, you'll spend all your mental energy trying to resurrect old thoughts instead of generating new ones. Writing ideas down also speeds up your thought processes and helps you to focus.[1]

This will be more fun than you think it will be because we're going to start out with things that are not serious. Start with a stack of notebook paper and use one side only. You'll be cutting the paper up into strips, so lines help. Think of all the secret fantasies you have had that would embarrass you if anybody found out about them. Writing one on every other line on your notepaper, list all the *crazy* things you would like to do before you die. Quantity breeds quality, so throw down absolutely everything that comes to mind. Don't waste time judging ideas, either. There is plenty of time for that later. Start with the really wild thoughts until your mind begins to loosen up. Eventually you will run out of dumb ideas and more sane ones will start to creep in as well.

Don't hold back *at all*. Have you secretly longed to be a movie star even though you are crippled by stage fright and you look like Garrison Keillor's ugly twin? Have you toyed with the idea of being the CEO of a Fortune 500 company? A world-class surgeon? Write it down. Have you dreamed of winning an Olympic gold medal but you're 63 years old and have bad arthritis? Sure, write it down. Competing in the Iditarod Alaskan Husky Race? Being an astronaut? Of course! When did the sky have to be the limit? The great philosophers certainly understood the importance of having wild visions. According to the Talmud, "Just as wheat is not without straw, so no dream is without some nonsense," so embrace the nonsense.

Be as specific as you can. Don't write just "travel" or "live abroad." Rather, write, "live in Venice for a year and take lessons in glass blowing." "Become a guide in the Amazon rain forest and establish an eco-tourist camp at the top of Angel Falls." You may want to become a real estate magnate and buy up Ed Rodeo Drive, or learn yoga and be a ballerina. Then you may want to learn to play the saxophone and be Miss America and take a trip around the world and bungee jump off the cliffs of Dover. How about getting a black belt in karate and beating up the girl who broke your brother's heart? Or talking your father into taking your mother on a second honeymoon? Put it all down. There are no limits.

Realistically, you know most of these things will never happen, but if you've fantasized about anything regularly, write it down anyway. You might as well have fun with it. As you write, you will reveal secret longings that aren't quite impossible, and some may actually be achievable, although you may never have considered them as such.

For instance, you actually can learn to sing or learn a foreign language or take a trip around the world or be the president of a company. You just never took that desire seriously enough to consider it before. If you think of a few things that you are already working toward, write those down, too. Leave none of your longings out. This will be the springboard for defining your Vision, and you don't want to shortchange yourself.

Many people, especially creative ones, have lots of crazy, unrealistic fantasies. By the time I've listed all the things I want to accomplish during my lifetime, I have ventured down so many rabbit holes that I may wind up playing croquet with the Queen of Hearts before I get anything accomplished.

Yet, the unrealistic Goals are valuable because they will give you a glimpse into your deep desires, as well as some of your weaknesses. If you have lots and lots of fanciful Goals, most of which may be unachievable in any practical way, what does it tell you about yourself? Maybe you are really creative. Maybe you like the idea of doing lots of different things, or you like excitement, or you like the idea of being "accomplished." Maybe you just aren't focused. Maybe your desires are so far away from your actual life, you discover that you are living way out in left field from where you should be. So even though you may list Goals that in the end you will never bother to try to achieve, by listing them, you can find a measure of self-awareness that will ultimately lead you toward your Vision.

After you have a list that's, oh, somewhere between the length of an Orangutan's arm and the Titanic, make 5 or 7 copies, and cut the paper up into strips, with one Goal written on each strip. Clip multiple copies of each Goal together. You should have quite a pile because you will have all those copies of every Goal that you have written. Put them in a pretty bowl and set them aside for now. We'll come back to them later.

Step 2: Prepare A Feast For the Soul

> *The guests are met, the feast is set*
> *May'st hear the merry din*
> ~Samuel Taylor Coleridge

Necessary Tools:
Thinking cap, quiet time to yourself, music, cup of tea (or similar), tape or sticky label, pen, bowl of Desires/Goals, a stack of saucers, plates, bowls, cups, etc.

Keep your bowl of desires set aside for a while. Now you are going to focus on some more serious matters. When you have some quiet time to yourself, take the time to begin the most nutritious meal you will ever make for yourself—your Soul Feast. Put on some classical music, brew a cup of tea, get comfortable, and begin thinking deeply about your values and needs.

What is it that makes life interesting and worthwhile for you? What appeals to you on such an intimate level that you would be miserable without it? What are the things you need in order to feel completely alive? Is it beauty? Love? Laughter? I call these things your "Soul Foods," because they are the things that your soul needs in order to feel fully nourished and satisfied.

Most of your "Soul Foods" are things with intrinsic value—things that are considered good in every culture, in every circumstance. The list is long and includes things from life and consciousness to self-expression and freedom. You might include some of your Life Worth Assets you identified in Chapter 3: things like strength, kindness, intelligence, a sense of humor, and so forth.

But you also may have a real yen for things with extrinsic value. These have value simply because people in a given society or community agree they have value. Money is one thing that has extrinsic value, as does status and glamour. Most of the things we associate with the trappings of the good life in our American culture are things with more extrinsic than intrinsic value, but it's ok if those things are important to you. As an ex-drama queen, too old and tired to relish drama anymore, I understand the importance of the adrenaline rush every now and then. You may thrive on drama, just as you may thrive on beauty or wealth or status or love.

Letting your mind go free, start listing possible Soul Foods—anything that comes to mind that you think is necessary for a quality life. There could be dozens, and here are some Soul Foods that you might start with. This list is by no means complete, so you will be adding more that apply uniquely to you, and of course, you won't bother with some that don't even smell yummy to your soul. I have underlined the ones that appeal most to me, so in the end, I would have 18 Soul Foods laid out for my Feast.

accomplishment	adventure	artistry	beauty
connectedness	compassion	control	fame
challenge	conformity	excellence	drama
excitement	family	freedom	home
friendship	status	intellectuality	love
individuality	laughter	leadership	joy
learning	luxury	music	nature
nurture	precision	pleasure	ro-
mance strength		security	spirit-
uality	wealth tranquility		

Write the name of each of your Soul Foods onto a sticky label or a piece of tape and tape it onto a pretty little saucer or plate. I'll have 18, so I'll need an assortment of teacups, bowls, plates, and saucers to hold them all. I personally think you should use your grandmother's Limoges china, as befitting the importance of your Soul Feast, but if you aren't lucky enough to have such, you can use plain old Dixie plates. Make room. Your kitchen table is about to get crowded.

Pick up your bowl full of desires/Goals and pull them out one at a time. As you read a Goal, think of it as a possible ingredient of a Soul Food. In other words, what deep value does that help to satisfy?

If you pick up "I want to live in Venice for a year and take lessons in glass blowing," ask yourself why you want to live in that city for that length of time and take up that particular activity. In doing so, you will understand that you might consider that an ingredient of "Adventure," "Beauty," "Learning, "Intellectuality," and "Status." Place the Goal into the corresponding Soul Food plate or saucer. You need multiple copies because most Goals won't fit into just one category. You'll need to put a copy in several vessels.

You should have some odd desires like: "I want to have an affair with Brad Pitt," or "I want to learn to levitate." But even those wild ideas actually are connected to some deeper need that you have. Maybe old Brad exemplifies your desire for love, or for status, for romance or drama or beauty. It probably wouldn't fit in tranquility, comedy, or intellectuality, but hey, we all have our own deep-seated motivations, so maybe it would. Try to put ALL the Goals, even the crazy ones, into a defining Soul Food plate or cup, being as honest as you can about yourself and your needs and passions.

If you don't have time to finish, it's fine to go away and think about this over the next few days. You can just stack up your saucers of Goals in a corner somewhere and come back to your Feast whenever you have time. Having them in view on the kitchen counter will be a little reminder for you to be thinking about what you want. Deliberately ponder which Goals really speak most true to your deepest desires, the ones that feed your soul.

Step 3: To Thine Own Self Be True

~Hamlet, William Shakespeare

Necessary Tools:
Thinking cap, music, piles of
Goals in their place settings

How are you doing? Have you actually started the exercises yet? If not, go back to Step 1 and really do it. It will help you think through this next step.

Your Vision is going to be unique to you, and no one can tell you what it is. Being true to yourself means that you realize that this is the only life you get, unless you are reincarnated, and even then, this is the only life you will have this time around, so this is all that counts. You don't need to waste any of it laboring under a false sense of self.

You can begin to know what is chaff and what is real when you deeply probe for what really matters to you. Here is where you may begin to discover that you really don't want to become an attorney or an engineer or a circus clown. You just had those Goals because your parents wanted you to have a particular career or because you like saying "I'm studying to be a nuclear physicist." Oops. If that's true, sounds like that Goal should go into the "Status" plate!

Don't throw away ANY Goals, no matter how crazy or embarrassing or ambitious they are. Some might not fit anywhere, no matter how much you try to put them into a Soul Food. If you can't figure out why on earth you wrote it down in the first place, make a "Miscellaneous" plate that you can deal with later. Or maybe you can come up with another Soul Food category that would incorporate them.

Once you have placed each of your slips of paper into their proper plates, you can throw out any excess copies. By now it will be obvious which values/desires are truly Soul Foods for you. Some plates will have a lot more "ingredients" than others, and some plates may be totally empty. Maybe you had some Soul Food plates prepared because those values just sounded good, or you thought they should be important to you, but now you find they aren't. If you have no Goals that reflect them, they don't apply to you. You can peel off the label and put those empty plates away now.

Think about the Soul Foods that have the most Goals, or "ingredients" supporting them, and see if you can combine some types of Soul Foods. If "Romance" has a pile of strips on it, ask yourself: Why are you drawn to romance? What is it about romance that appeals to you? Is it really the desire for beauty? Or is it love? What does romance mean to you? Does it mean hot sex in the hot tub? My husband would say YES! and I would poke him in the ribs with my elbow.

To me, romance means a scene from a 40s movie—candles and dancing in the moonlight to beautiful, sexy music, and air perfumed with roses and the sound of wind dancing in the trees. And of course there has to be a guy I love there, too, who also loves me, and who is really good looking and is smart and funny and a great conversationalist who can talk about Marlowe and Kant and can adequately explain the theory of relativity. He'll be able to point out the Crab Nebula and tell me the legends associated with it. He also can sing like Frank Sinatra and dance like Gene Kelly and loves to indulge my every whim.

Needless to say, I'm asking a bit much of my man, and if I don't compromise a bit, I'll never have my brand of a perfectly romantic evening. But by the time I am done weeding through what it is about romance that appeals to me, I find that it's beauty, intellectuality, love, nature, music, and connectedness. I can now actually get rid of the "Romance" category because it really breaks down to those more specific measures.

As you delve into all this, you're going to find out some things about yourself that you don't find particularly attractive. Let's say one of your Goals is "I want to feed poison to the girl who stole my guy." Fair enough. She probably deserves it, and it might actually make you feel better for a minute or two to contemplate the idea of her writhing on the floor in hideous pain.

But when you try to put that ingredient into a Soul Food, you probably will discover that "Vengeance" doesn't sit on the soul's stomach well, and it might conflict with other insights that you have of yourself. In reality, your desire to feed the bitch poison probably comes from a different set of motivators, and that may really fit in a convoluted way under "Love" or "Security" or "Connectedness." She has stolen your lover, and that has made you feel vulnerable, worthless, and insecure. It has made you grieve, has taken away your joy, and so forth. It is the pain of all these things that makes you want to slap the little slut and get revenge.

If you step back a bit more, you may find that the desire for revenge comes directly out of pain, and if you really think about that, pain probably is not something that you particularly want to embrace. Wouldn't you rather embrace love or security or connectedness? The things that were lost are really more important to you than the pain that rushed in to fill the void. You would rather get those lovely things back than live with pain any more than you have to.

At this point, you have some choices. First, you can keep the Goal as it is: You *really do* want revenge. You may have to get another plate.

Second: You can modify the Goal, making it conform to the things you really want: You want to find a fantastic man who loves you just as you are and who will be so faithful that you don't have to worry about other women.

Keep weeding through, keep refining. Eventually, you will find that you have considered and distilled your Goals so well that you can begin to define the essential *you*—what appeals to you on the most intimate level—in other words, what nourishes your soul.

Step 4: Separate Vision from Noise

*Noise is the most impertinent of all forms of
interruption. It is not only an interruption,
but is also a disruption of thought.*

~Arthur Schopenhauer

Necessary Tools:
*Thinking cap, piles of Goals , fresh
paper, pen, music, another cup of tea*

When you have finished distilling, modifying, and
refining your deep desires, you will begin to feel that you
pretty much fully know yourself. Now it's time to establish
the framework by which you can begin to see how to find
your best life—your Queendom, based upon the Dreams
that you have defined as quintessentially yours.

Have you actually begun to write yet? Merely doing
this in your head is not much better than nothing, and when
you honor your Desires by writing them down, your chances
of achieving them goes up about a zillion percent. Besides,
it's much easier to keep it all straight if you organize your
thoughts. Keep that pen in hand!

Now, get a fresh piece of paper. Beginning at the top,
but not at the very tippy top—you need to save about 2
inches for what goes above that, which I will discuss later.
Draw a vertical line down the middle of the paper and at the
sort-of-top and

on the left side write   and   on the right side write

VISION   NOISE

Below <u>VISION</u>, write a
statement which articu-
lates what you have
learned about yourself: a

summation of all the Soul Foods that were most supported by your Goals. It probably will be incomplete, but you can start a tentative VISION Statement that might look like this:

A. "I want to live a full, rich life, full of laughter, deep spirituality, beauty, and love. I want to nurture and cherish others, particularly my own children and one man. I want to make a difference in the world in a small (or large) way by raising healthy, happy children who grow into responsible, loving adults. I want to have some quiet, mostly intellectual adventures, but basically, I want to live serenely and peacefully."

OR your VISION statement might say:

B. "I want to live life TO THE HILT! I want fame, fortune, excitement, glamour, and lots of love. I want people to look up to me and adore me, and I want to adore others just as much. I hope to be too busy having adventures to worry about having children, or even a single relationship. My freedom is too important to me to be tied down to anyone. I want to be remembered for the great things I have accomplished in this life."

You can put away your plates and saucers now, but you need to keep your strips of Goals, and maybe you should make yourself another cup of tea, because you're still going to need some wisdom, which I have heard that tea provides. You may still have some Goals in there that might not be terribly attractive, that make you seem shallow or petty or self-obsessed. That's ok. We all are sometimes shallow and petty and self-obsessed. Some of those Goals might be clearly unachievable. Leave those in there for now, too. They are still valuable.

Pick up a Goal and read it. Do you still like it? Does it feed your soul? If so, great. Place it on your piece of paper underneath the word "VISION." Do you find yourself having second thoughts about the Goal? Some Goals may be ones that you thought you wanted to achieve, but as it turns out, they were really only what you *thought* you wanted or what other people thought you should have. Such a Rider does not belong in your Queendom, and, in fact, is a traitor to your cause. The desires that are not a part of your soul's true longings will distract you from fulfilling your Vision. If you let them, they will pull you into a direction that you really don't need or want to be going.

Did you write down a Goal of getting a fancy new car, but you now realize that is your boyfriend's idea of what you should want? What you *really* want has nothing to do with a cool new car. Maybe your soul yearns to find a place where you can be constantly immersed in beauty and knowledge. Maybe you really want to quit your job and move to London to work in the Victoria and Albert museum.

Now this is important, so pay attention: Once you understand that the car, or whatever the "false" Goal is will not feed your soul, you can see that it might actually sabotage your Queendom by directing you toward a life you are not satisfied with. That Goal does not fit in your Vision.

Let it go! It wasn't a true desire, but rather a pesky noise that hummed on the periphery of your consciousness, or perhaps even in the center of it and has caused you to lose your focus on what you really wanted. Simply place that undesirable Goal in the Noise category. Now it is no longer your Goal, and you can relieve yourself of even the possibility of trying to achieve it. Once you become free of it, you can concentrate on the real stuff.

Let's say your Vision is the first one, or A, above. But one of your Goals is "I want to have an affair with Brad Pitt." Damn, that keeps cropping up, doesn't it? Ask yourself: How will having an affair with Brad Pitt help me realize my Vision of loving and nurturing one man? Sorry, it doesn't. At least not as far as I can figure it, no matter how I try to twist the logic. The sad truth is, Brad probably should go off to the NOISE side. Sorry Brad. Your loss. By having the affair with Brad, or anyone, you risk destroying the basic fabric of your Vision, and once your Vision becomes undermined, you lose your happiness. Brad and company do not fit in your Queendom. You need to go back and figure out why he keeps coming into this picture.

Is it that the man you are with right now isn't doing for you what you had hoped he might be doing? That may not be a reason to trade him in for Brad. It may just be a screaming notice that you need to repair your relationship. Keep tinkering. You may need to add an additional Goal: "Develop a better relationship with my husband." Ultimately, ALL your Goals should fit within your Vision, and they should line up perfectly. If you still want to keep some Goals that don't fit, adjust your Vision statement so that you have no inconsistencies between your values and your desires.

There are other things that are putting Noise into your life that were not on your list of Goals. That's all the other activities or demands that clutter your life and your psyche that cause you to lose sight of what is important. The career path you are on right now might actually be Noise. Is what you are doing at your job in conflict with your deep, soul satisfying Vision? If not, I'm not suggesting that you march in to work tomorrow, screaming, "I QUIT!" I'm just suggesting you need to realize that there may be something about your job that needs to be rethought and adjusted. It's possible that you can rethink your career choice so that it more perfectly fits into your Vision.

Maybe you are a corporate attorney, but you have found that, aside from the great salary, there isn't much about it that you really like. You'd rather be working with nonprofit organizations. But you have student debt to pay off, and it looks as if you will never be able to afford to do what you really want. Forget all that. Just concentrate on what you want and why you want it. Later, you'll discover strategies to overcome the problems. Right now, you just want to concentrate on your deepest longings, without the distraction of trying to figure out how to reach them.

Some things to be listed on the Noise side might involve plans your boyfriend or your best friends have made for you. It might be plans you are making which are leading you in the wrong direction. Anything that does not directly contribute toward creating a life that fulfills your Vision should be moved over or entered in the column under NOISE.

One caveat here: If you're very young, you may have fancies that appeal to you which are unsuitable for you. Don't scorn the counsel of your parents or trusted friends who may know you better than you know yourself, because they may understand your gifts more than you do. Mary Elizabeth "knew" she wanted to be a doctor by the time she was in the fifth grade. As her parents, we didn't want to discourage her, but we saw that her gifts lay in other directions. She was built to be an artist, not a scientist. Consequently, while we didn't actually discourage her from pursuing a career in medicine, we tended to nudge her in the direction of art and literature. She figured it out on her own when she hit Organic Chemistry in her junior year of college and met an art professor who nurtured her real talent. Sometimes your parents really do know what's best!

Step 5: Find the Greater Good and Line 'em up

Necessary Tools:
Thinking cap, music, file cards, pen,
paper outlining VISION and NOISE

The next step is to test your Vision and your Goals against a higher standard. I told you to leave a space at the top of the page, above VISION. Take the opportunity to step back a bit further and examine yourself in a larger context. At the very tippy top of the page, directly above VISION, write another phrase that can help you think about the really big picture and which will help you come to terms with your deepest values. At the tippy top of my list I have written

"GOD'S HEART." The way I see it, if it doesn't fit into God's heart—in other words, if it isn't intrinsically good, and doesn't ultimately contribute to good in some way—it has no business being in my Vision or my Goals or anything that goes in line below those.

You may want to use a different phrase to define an all-encompassing idea, something like "HARMONY WITH THE UNIVERSE" or some such. By using the term "GOD'S HEART," it gives me a shortcut. I don't know exactly what's in God's heart, but I know it contains basic core values such as honesty, integrity, and rightness. We usually instinctively know what these things are because they have been instilled in us from infancy.

It is impossible to live well if you try to operate outside the core value of goodness. You can try to thwart those old morality "rules" all day long, but all you will ever succeed in doing is making yourself and all those around you miserable. Hatred, envy, greed, all those things we have been taught to avoid for a good reason. Those things ruin lives, and there is no way around it. In order to find happiness, in order to truly live well, you must seek after things that are good, eternal, and inherently "right." The other direction leads to madness and misery.

I'm not going to belabor this because I am certain that if you cared enough about your life to pick up this book, we have no quarrel. The job now is to make sure your VISION and your Goals completely conform and fit within the framework of universal goodness. Your Queendom deserves no less.

Look at your Vision statement again. Do you need to change it in any way to make it fit into God's Heart? Once it does fit, let's turn back to another examination of your Goals. Keep shifting them around, maybe rewriting a few, determining if they actually fit under your Vision and God's

Heart, or if they more properly should be shuttled over to the Noise side. Once you've spent some time doing this, you should have a pretty good list of things you want to accomplish in your life.

Brad is probably gone by now, as is the poisoning of the home wrecker. Some that remain in the "keep" pile may still be farfetched, but that's ok. Keep them in there for now, because they may actually survive the next few tests, or they may evolve into Goals that feed your soul but will be easier to accomplish. Even the most ambitious Dreams can be accomplished with the right tools, as long as they fit into the column on the left side of your VISION page.

By now your little strips of paper are probably getting a little ratty looking, now that you've caressed and mauled them repeatedly. At this point, you can transfer your Goals to file cards—one per card. As you write them, stack them up on your Vision sheet. At the top of the list and to the left of the page is

GOD'S HEART

If you want, list all the intrinsic values that describe what you think are in God's heart: Truth, justice, goodness, etc.

Underneath that is:

VISION on the left	and	**NOISE** on the right
All your Goals, the realistic and unrealistic ones, that fit within your VISION and in God's HEART should be written on cards and placed onto the page here.		All the Goals and the hindrances in your current situation that prevent you from living the life you want should be written on cards and stacked up here.

As time goes by, you will add some things to both the Vision and the Noise sections.

Check your Vision again. Are you sure it fits in God's Heart? Yes? Good. Now, pick up your first Goal. Does that fit your Vision, even though it may be farfetched? Yes? Great. Place it on the Vision side. You're rolling now.

On my list are some doozies, and most of them are totally unrealistic. I have always wanted to hike the Appalachian Trail. I love the mountains, and there is a romance about the AT that draws me to it. Of course, I want this book to affect the lives of millions. I also have "Run with the Bulls in Pamplona, Spain," on my list, along with getting my written, but unpublished novel into circulation and made into a movie, living in Florence for a few months, owning a house in Costa Rica, learning several languages, discovering a cure for cancer, banishing evil from the planet, taking up a musical instrument, flying to the moon. . . . Absolutely all these fit perfectly into my Vision for myself and make up a pretty cozy, happy little Queendom. Each one fulfills a desire for adventure, intellectuality, beauty, and so forth. They also fit into my definition of God's Heart; so theoretically, they are great Goals for me. So let's go for it!

What's next? The big question: What do I need to do in order to actually begin to accomplish these Goals?

CHAPTER 7

MAKING IT HAPPEN

Go confidently in the direction of your dreams.
Live the life you have imagined.
~Henry David Thoreau

One of my clients, whom I love because he is both kind and honest, recently gave me a hard talking to. Frankly, he really didn't like all the tough questions I was asking him which forced him to understand himself and his desires. He said, "When you look at yourself in the mirror and say, 'there's nobody else here and you have to drop all pretentions and be completely honest with yourself about who you really are and what you really want and what you really can do,' that's hard. And it can be painful."

No kidding it's hard. After all, blissful embracing of possibilities is a lot easier than facing what needs to be done, and by extension, admitting to one's limitations. As I work with my financial planning clients, most of them are perfectly happy when we are discussing all the hopes and Dreams they have. But at some point, they begin to realize where all this dreaming is leading, and they start worrying about what that means.

There are two places where people get flat-out scared. The first scary place comes when they realize that they may not have enough resources to do the ordinary things they said they wanted to do. They may be far short in their savings for their retirement or their children's college tuition costs, so now they face the ugly reality that they are going to have to drastically change their behavior if they are to realize their hopes and ambitions.

Deborah Griffitts Hining

The second place where people get scared is when they realize they *do* have the resources to do the *extraordinary* things they said they wanted to do. If someone tells me she dreams of leaving her $100,000 per year job to join the Peace Corps for two years, for some reason she is likely to be astonished when I say, "Yes, we can make that happen. I just need to restructure your portfolio a bit. When do you want to leave?" You can see the sudden fear come into her eyes as she starts thinking about what a "crazy" notion that is.

When people begin envisioning the real possibility that they might do something extraordinary, they realize that their lives will change, perhaps drastically and permanently.

What are they opening themselves up to? What new circumstances will they have to face? What if they get into this new situation and discover they don't like it? How different will this new direction be than the comfortable life they are used to?

It's hard to imagine how you will face any new reality, and how much you will be forced to change and grow. How much work will it take to whip yourself into good enough shape to do more and be more? At this point, you begin to understand why Money is among the least of the Life Worth Assets you will need to accomplish your Dreams. More important are Assets like Flexibility, Creativity, Ambition, Drive, and who-knows-what else. Maybe you don't have enough of these Assets in your Life Worth Balance to do what you say you want to do. What if you have more Liabilities than you thought you had? These, after all, are hindrances that can stall your progress, or can keep you from adapting to your new reality.

If you are going to build a life that is rich and worthwhile, the life you say you want, you may have to start either eliminating those liabilities or increasing your assets.

Fortunately, there is a way to do that, if you can look at yourself honestly and determine to make the effort. You have to step away from dreaming and theoretical introspection and toward the practical matter of work to be done to mold your Queendom the way you want it.

Now that you have a good idea of what things you want to have and to accomplish, you need to actually do what it takes to make it all happen, and that takes work that you may not be used to. Although we are frantically busy most of the time, in reality we've let ourselves become lazy about how to approach living. Much of what we get caught up in has just happened willy-nilly: either someone told us what to do, and we did it, or we did things in response to spur of the moment circumstances and on factors which may not have been all that meaningful.

What are you doing with your life right now? What job do you have, what friends, where do you live? Did you deliberately choose these, and do you feel you have done the right things?

When I graduated from high school, I went to college at the University of Tennessee. While I was there, some very important things happened which irrevocably shaped my life. I met Mike, chose Theatre as my major, met a professor who thought I was smart and encouraged me to go to graduate school. That professor suggested I go to LSU, and so I didn't bother checking out any other graduate programs. I just packed up and moved to Baton Rouge, where another whole set of circumstances presented themselves. They, in turn, changed the direction of my life further.

Why did I go to UT? Because it was close to home and cheap, and all my friends were going there. I didn't have to think in order to make the choice. Why did a lot of my friends choose UT? Because it was considered one of the biggest party schools in the South. Why did I go to LSU?

Because my professor went there and liked a certain professor, and that was good enough for me. Now there are some excellent reasons for choosing the path that will determine the direction of the rest of my life!

I was lucky. All those mindlessly made decisions turned out happily, but not every decision I have made without considering them have not. Now that I am older and wiser, I tend to think through decisions a bit more carefully, for I realize that every choice I make changes the future, possibly irrevocably.

I'm not saying we should belabor every decision. Far from it. If we tried to think through every long-term consequence of every action that we are faced with, life would end up being *waaay* too serious. It would be agony to try to think through every ramification, to make sure that in every instance we make the right choices for the right reasons with the best possible outcomes.

The way to keep it from being such an issue, but still make choices that will more or less be right for you, is to *first* make decisions on what your life should look like—that is, find your Vision. Defining your Vision and determining to work toward it means that when you are at a crossroads, you can head in the right general direction. You already know your destination: your Queendom is right there in front of you! And you know not to take a path that leads away from it.

If you live on the East Coast and you want to go to San Francisco, you probably will have the sense to head west. Even if you take a little detour to see the giant chicken just outside Kalona, Iowa, you are likely to get back onto the highway headed west again.

If you just jump in the car without having first dreamed up a destination, there's no telling where you'll end up. It isn't enough to say, "I gotta get out of this one-horse town." If you do, chances are, your final destination will not be the same one you would have come to if you had already decided on it. Most likely it won't be as nice as one you take the trouble to plan for. You may even just spend your life wandering around in circles.

Even if you plan carefully, life is going to throw enough curves at you so that you may not arrive at the pre-determined destination. But you'll be closer than you would have been if you had not made deliberate choices. If you planned on San Francisco, but end up in Sausalito or Napa, you're probably not going to be very disappointed, like you would be if you landed in Moose hide Junction, Alaska, or Guantanamo, Cuba. And of course, once you figure out where you are in relation to where you want to be, it's not such a hard thing to adjust your course southward if San Francisco is what you truly want.

Rather than deciding which school to attend, which groups to join, which job to take, or even whether to go to school or join a group or take a job at all, you should have already made some decisions about what your soul needs. You should be able to say something like: "I really love taking care of people and seeing bodies heal. I would like to pursue a career in medicine." Then seek out your options for activities/job opportunities/classes that will allow you to learn about medicine and/or prepare you for medical school. You will still make bad choices now and then, but you'll at least you'll know what your Queendom looks like and what it is likely to take to build it.

HORSES

A horse! A horse! My kingdom for a horse!
~ Richard III, by William Shakespeare

Once you have identified some Goals that could help you realize your Vision, you need to find a way to accomplish them. You must develop Strategies that will help you get there. Strategies are tasks that must be completed before you can achieve any Goal. They are your Horses—the work animal of this process. Trying to reach Goals without strategies is like trying to fight a battle on foot. You might as well face the fact that you're not getting anywhere, and you probably will get trampled.

> When Richard III was unseated in the Battle of Bosworth, he desperately needed to get another horse so he could get back to fighting. He didn't find a horse, and because he was on foot and vulnerable, he was ultimately killed, and his kingdom was truly lost. He was the last king in the line of York, so the whole dynasty disappeared, all because poor old Richie couldn't take care of his horse!

Let's start looking at our Goals one at a time, and determine what has to be done, what Strategies we can employ to help us reach each of them. Pick up your stack of Goal cards and read the first one.

Mine is: "Run with the bulls in Pamplona, Spain." I actually want to do this because it is on my son George's list, and if he goes, I want to be along to keep him as safe as I can. I figure it would also be a great bonding experience. Fits into my Vision of adventure, family, connectedness, and in a strange way, intellectuality. I certainly would learn something new if I did it! God probably would object to the treatment of the bulls, but mostly I think he would just roll his eyes. He's seen worse.

So what would it take to accomplish this Goal? What Strategies do I need to employ to make it happen?

Strategy 1: Figure out a way to do it without getting killed or maimed.

Oh, I got that one covered. The way to do it safely would be to start out in the very front of the pack, about, oh, a mile or two in front of the bulls, and if the bulls, or even if any of the other runners, should happen to get within earshot, I would leap over the barrier to safety, dragging George with me, and hunker down there until all the excitement had passed. Then I could get back on course and bring up the rear of the procession, well behind the last bull. Smart, huh? I used my Life Worth Assets, Creativity and Common Sense to come up with that one. I am so brilliant!

Strategy 2: Examine the course to make sure I understand where the barriers are, and what I have to look for to make sure I always have an escape route. So, Johnny-on-the-spot, I looked it up on Google to plot my course.

Very interesting. Those streets are narrow! Barriers exist only at some places, and the only way to escape for most of the course is to climb a wall. I mean, climb up the face of a stone house! There are lots of pictures on the site showing people running, but none of them are middle aged, out-of-shape American ladies. They are all young, male, and very fit.

Oh, dear, I'm having second thoughts about that Goal.

Maybe I could actually do it, but I don't like the idea of making a spectacle of myself in front of those crowds. I imagine myself very winded, terrified, but pretending to be brave, tottering along with those bandana wearing, macho, mustachioed young men. Would that help me fulfill my Vision of living honestly, with truth and purpose? I don't think so! I would be a farce, and probably go down in the annals of Pamplona history as the old nutcase who pretended to run with the bulls.

This isn't such a good idea. Honestly, I really don't have enough Life Worth Assets to make this happen, and I am not willing to do what it takes to increase them as much as I need to. In truth, that is because it really isn't my Dream—it is George's, and as I think about what it would take to accomplish this, I come up pretty short. Sadly, I think I am going to have to move this goal over to the NOISE column!

And so I do. But at least I have honored that desire by taking it seriously and examining it, and I gave it a chance to take root and flower. I gave myself the chance to really discover if it was something I wanted to choose or not. If I abandon that Dream, I do it deliberately, knowing that I have done it consciously and actively, and I can give it a decent send-off. Once it's gone, I can quit wasting time fantasizing about it and can put my precious resources to better use finding a Goal which would help me realize my Vision of connectedness with my child without risking life, limb, and self-respect.

The fact is, after close examination, I realize that I never wanted to actually run with the bulls, although it would be fun to have run with them, and it took my examining that desire closely to come to that realization. It sure would be a nice conversation starter to be at a fancy party with a bunch of people I would love to impress, and when someone comments on how good the tapas are or how nice the weather is, be able to say (very casually, of course), "Oh, that reminds me. Last summer, when I was running with the bulls in Pamplona, I bumped into the most amazing person..." I can just imagine the pause in the conversation, where everyone looks at me with admiration.

Yes, having done wonderful, exciting things is much easier than doing what it takes to actually do them. Like a lot of optimists, I pretty much overload myself when it comes to setting down Life Goals, and like a lot of lazy people, I don't do much about accomplishing them. Sadly, the fact is, it's easy to dream big if all you are doing is dreaming. But spending all your time dreaming keeps you from actually doing, as Walter Mitty proved. Your desires must be real and important enough so that you will have the willingness to follow through, the courage and tenacity it takes to make things happen.

So what's my problem? Some people do make an ambitious list of the things they want to do, and sometimes they manage to accomplish all of them, even the ones that seem farfetched. What's the difference between lazy but optimistic me and the ambitious and optimistic others who manage to do everything from starring in a movie to winning the Nobel prize?

It's simple. I lack either the talent, ambition, or proper knowledge to accomplish most of my Goals. Maybe I lack all three. I don't have enough Life Worth assets to "purchase" the Goals I say I want. I am not committed enough to do battle for them.

You may have heard about people who have done extraordinary things and have awed you with their drive, passion, and resourcefulness. If you want to be amazed by someone's intense purpose of will, read the biographies of Rosa Parks, the mother of the Civil Rights movement, or the 1940s actress Hedy Lamarr, who developed important technology and invented a secret communication system to thwart the Nazis during World War II, [1] or Jane Goodall, the anthropologist who has spent most of her life studying and living among chimpanzees. These were/are extraordinary people with extraordinary passion and extraordinary ambition. Unfortunately, when I read about them, I am not really inspired. Rather than giving me courage and initiative, these people make me feel tired, puny, and hopeless.

I don't like it when I realize what a wuss I am, too lazy to get up off my fat duff and do something worthwhile. So why am I not out there, saving the world from Nazis, helping to bring justice to a downtrodden people, dedicating my life to an important cause, leading warriors into battle to save the Queendom? Because I'm stupid and lazy and selfish, that's why. I am worthless. Pitiful. Obviously I will never accomplish anything worthwhile, so I think I'll watch "Three's Company" reruns and eat fudge. Maybe curl up with a bottle of vodka.

You may identify with this. You might have the best of intentions, but somehow, when you go home at night, tired after a day of plowing, it's much easier to flip on the TV and eat peanut butter out of the jar than it is to get yourself psyched up enough to do the research, the training, the mental exercise it will take to really accomplish something. Having run with the bulls is easier than actually running, but eating a gallon of Rocky Road ice cream is easier than having eaten it. So Rocky Road it is! At least I'm doing something that gives me instant gratification, and I can ignore the impending consequences for a while.

Take heart. If you are too lazy or uneducated or unskilled enough to do what it takes to become a world class cellist or the head of a Fortune 500 company or the next Madame Curie, that doesn't mean you aren't going to live a glorious, fulfilled life, full of pleasure and adventure, love and goodness. You just have to find the things which are important enough to you that you actually want do them, and you have to take the next step: to get organized and gather the right tools which will allow you to proceed.

You might need to scale down a bit, but once you learn to embrace the real core of what you are, you can reach your full potential, no matter how large or small that may be. It's ok to be a peasant or a very tiny cog in a very tiny machine within the large machine of this world, and it's ok to do only one spectacular (or merely interesting) thing in your whole life. The trick is to know yourself, finding the things you can do, and are willing to do, as long as they are things that feed your soul. (It also hinges on how well you take care of your Horseshoes and Nails, but that's a discussion for the next chapters).

You need to discover the things that exist in your Queendom and understand where you draw the line of what you are willing to do to make them real. Ok, so let me pick myself up out of the gutter of self-loathing and pity, and look at another Goal that might make more sense than racing through the streets of Pamplona with the bulls snorting at my heels:

"I want to hike the Appalachian Trail." Ok, great Goal. It fits within my Vision and helps to feed my soul. I'm sure God would approve. Now, what, exactly do I need to do before I can make the trip?

I have hiked several portions of the AT, so I have an inkling of what it would take to prepare to hike from Georgia to Maine along the high, rugged back of the Appalachian mountains. What Strategies do I need to employ to get myself into shape enough to drag myself 2,175 miles up and down mountains, slogging through mud, rain, heat, flies, mosquitoes, sleeping on the ground, hauling all my food and supplies on my back?

Uhmmmm. . . . Well, just off the top of my head: I would need to buy a lot of gear, and I should get my hiking boots early so I can break them in well before the trip begins. I probably should find someone to go along with me. And arrange to take enough time off work. I would have to figure out just when to start in order to take advantage of weather conditions, timing it so that I left Springer Mountain in Georgia as soon as it warms up enough to travel. I also must get a plan for making it from one shelter to another within certain time frames so that I could get to Katahdin, Maine before the first real snowfall.

And I guess I have to get my knees replaced. They already sound like fresh Rice Krispies in milk when I walk up the stairs, so I don't think they would make the trip without artificial aid. I also need to go through an extreme exercise regimen where I develop enough muscles and stamina to carry a 30 pound pack. . . .

Is this sounding like work to you? Unfortunately, if you are going to live a life actually doing the things you think you want to do, you have to do some hard work. What Goals do you have sitting in your heart or mind that you want to accomplish, but you aren't sure you want to do the work it takes? Are you like me in that you want to have done the equivalent of *having hiked* the Appalachian Trail, but, after you really think about it, you aren't so sure you want to actually *hike it?* Sure, you do! So now is the time to really examine those Goals and decide to fish or cut bait. Do you want to do it or not?

I'd love to be able to remember the high places, the astonishing views, the moments of spiritual awareness that transport me into the giddy heights that doing something really wonderful provides. The reality of laying my creaky old joints on the hard, cold ground after dragging myself up a mountain and eating reconstituted oatmeal for breakfast for days on end really doesn't appeal to me very much. Having the memories and being able to brag about having been so brave and strong and adventurous is much more appealing.

Could I take on the trail if I really wanted to? Yeeeeeesss, I guess I could, but frankly, it would take more than I am willing to do. This is getting uncomfortable, because I am truly reluctant to give up that shining Dream and move it to the Noise side. You, too, no doubt have some longstanding, but clearly unachievable, desires that really sing to you about which you are ambivalent. If you have such a dilemma, take the time to figure out why.

I want to hike the Appalachian Trail because I love the mountains, and I love walking in them. But maybe it's the mountains I need to think about, not just the AT. Sure there are stunning views and special places on the AT, but there are such places in all the mountains. I've seen some of them, and I know what it feels like to stand at the top of a "generic" mountain ridge with the morning mist swirling up from the valley floor and smell the laurel as the sun creeps up the side of the mountain. I know how it feels to have my spirit swell with the knowledge God is there and to be thankful for such things as sunshine and mist and green and blue vistas that spread out as far as I can see. I know how sweet it is to stand beside someone I love and share the sense of the wind on our faces and the warming sun as we listen to the mockingbird in the rhododendron. Those perfect moments are the ones that nourish my soul and give me a glimpse into my Queendom. It sickens me to think about letting such a Dream go. Your Queendom holds such tantalizing vistas as well, and you know you will feel impoverished if you give them up.

What part of the Dream do you hate to give up, and what part are you happy to ditch? Reflecting on this, I realize it's not the act of hiking the AT that calls me.

Deborah Griffitts Hining

Rather, it's the beauty of the mountains, the spiritual lift, and the moments of spectacular quiet by the side of someone I care about. My soul can actually be fed, and fed well, with smaller, less grandiose goals. I need to quit lying to myself about what I really want.

Obviously, I need to go back and revisit my Vision and try to discover what I can do to reach it without getting my knees replaced.

VISION:

I want to be surrounded by beauty and by people I love, and to live truthfully, with deep spiritually. I want to continue learning my whole life, and I want to help people reach more of their full potential. I want to connect with others, and have interesting and fun adventures with them.

Pretty tame stuff. I don't have any Vision to be rich or famous or fabulously accomplished. I just want life to be sweet, easy, and interesting, and I want to leave the world a better place than it was when I entered it. So what's the deal with wanting to hike the AT, or run with the bulls, or become a ballerina or go to the moon? Those are just fancies that flirt with my vision of peace, sweetness, beauty, adventure, love and truth. They aren't really necessary to fulfill the Vision.

Yes, I like adventure. I like to think of myself as someone who rides life like it's a wild beast, letting it fling me around and knowing what it feels like to live big and bold. But honestly, bigness and boldness is usually more trouble than I care to deal with. What I really want is adventures that are fun, not stressful, and with someone I love, who shares my view of truth and beauty.

Living a big, bold life all alone would be like wearing a gaudy garment all by myself that is designed for two or more people. Some of those ambitious goals I have written down would just hang on me and drag the ground, tripping me up and making me stumble and grope. As much as I would like to, I'm not cut out to run with bulls or conquer mountains. I am cut out to have smaller adventures with others so we can take care of each other while enjoying it together.

This realization means I must go back and understand that my Queendom means love, beauty, and connectedness are my top priorities, not the physical sensation of slogging up a muddy trail and camping on the hard ground in the rain, no matter how great the view from the top, no matter how big the bragging rights.

So we must determine what we can do and are willing to do that will still feed our souls.

Ah ha! I just figured out that I can make regular trips to the mountains with my husband or children or good friends and just take day hikes along lovely trails! It doesn't have to be the AT. Wouldn't I rather take shorter hikes that are beautiful and let my soul snack on smaller bites? I don't need the whole 5 course meal at one go! And, boy, am I breathing a sigh of relief right now! Why did I think I had to drive myself so hard?

Now I can quit lying to myself that I am going to make the whole trek one day. The fact that the whole AT was on my list made it a Noise that distracted me from focusing on more realistic things. As long as I entertained the idea of hiking The Trail, it was a roadblock rather than an inspiration. I spent a lot of time and energy fantasizing about it, when I could have been using precious resources working toward doing something that is actually possible for me! Until I had this epiphany, I was more likely to go to the mall and eat fried dough than I was to plan for the more achievable Goal of taking shorter hikes regularly.

We all have many Goals that do not really fit directly into our Visions, but only sit around the edges of it. They may inherently incorporate pieces of our Vision, but they are not the means to actually achieving it fully. What Goals do you have which need to be modified to fit your Vision so they won't require resources you don't have? How can you change impossible Goals so that you will be willing and able to see them through?

Once you determine that, write the new Goal on your file card. Mine is: "Make at least 10 day hikes every year with Mike/my children/good friends, beginning this month." This new Goal better fulfills my Vision. I have shifted the emphasis from the activity of specifically hiking *The Trail* to spending meaningful time in the mountains on *a* trail with someone I love.

On the back of your Goal card, list the strategies you must take to reach the goal, and then decide if you can do all of them:

1. "Ask the people I want to join me when they can make the trip so we can set the dates."

2. "Buy some books and surf the net to decide which trails to hike."

3. "Get any equipment I will need ready and start working out more regularly."

4. "Make weekend trips to the mountains and take long walks whenever I can."

(Sub strategy: "Plan for a trip to the mountains next weekend, and schedule several more in the calendar right now.")

Boy, am I feeling better about myself! I can feel the excitement bubble up. The mountains sing to me! I'm actually going to do it because I actually can do it. I have the resources that it takes—Vision, Desire, Drive, Time on the weekends, enough Energy—and I realize that I must do it *now*. Why didn't I do this before? Because when I thought about hiking, I thought I had to do the AT, and that overwhelmed me so much, I either went shopping or reached for the full fat chocolate caramel mocha fudge ice cream.

Bits and Bites

A Vision, any Vision that is worthwhile, requires work to achieve, and the work should be done in bits that you can bite off and achieve one at a time. By now you may have noticed that you have some short term, medium term, and long term Goals. You can't achieve all of them at once, or even work toward all of them at once. Think of approaching your Goals as triage, working on the ones that are your most important Soul Food ingredients first, and then working your way down. If you determine to work daily on one short term, one medium term, and one long term Goal, and focus your energies on it, you will have better success.

Let's say you have picked:

Short term goal: Join a soccer league

Strategies would be pretty easy. Just do it!

Medium term goal: Take a whale watching canoe trip off the coast of Seattle.

Here are a few of the many strategies you need to deal with. I have them in no particular order.

Strategies:

1. Decide whether to do it alone or with friends (ask the friends)

2. Determine how much it will cost

3. Make arrangements to go.

You may hit a snag at #2. Maybe at this point you discover that such a trip will be much more expensive than you thought it would be. You simply don't have enough money to cover all the costs. That's a typical excuse not to do it—that and the fact that you can't find any friends who will go with you once they see how much it costs. Now you need to find a way to overcome the problem, and that will require another whole set of Strategies. But you can still do it, if you really want to. Resources other than money can get you in that canoe to see those whales. But what other resources do you have, and how do you use them?

Remember those Life Worth Assets we discussed in Chapter 4? Well, now is the time to draw on them, when you can't just pick up the checkbook and write the check to cover the cost of the whale watching expedition or whatever it is that is that you really want to do. What Assets do you have that will help you achieve that Dream anyway?

First, let's take a look at what you have: Social Currency; Ambition & Drive; Imagination & Creativity; and good old Time are probably what's going to get you to the whales' playground. If you have enough of these Assets, you can get all the Knowledge, Money, and other Life Worth Assets you could possibly need.

Do you really want to go whale watching? It is a true Desire, or just a passing fancy that would be nice, but really isn't necessary to feed your soul? Are you willing to work to make this happen? If so, you have your first Life Worth Asset, Ambition & Drive, at the ready to carry you forward. Now let's get your Creativity into play and figure out what Actions you can take to accomplish this Dream, even though you don't have the money it costs to do it the conventional way.

It's fun to be creative, and it's amazing what ideas you can come up with if you just let your Imagination have free rein. To get those creative juices raining, first define the problem: "I want to go to Washington State to see the whales. The cost to fly from Raleigh-Durham to Seattle, and hotel accommodations (for a shared room) for a week, and the cost of the tour will be about $600. Food will cost another $250, if we eat on the cheap, so we will need about $850 per person for a week of whale watching. I have only $400. How can I either raise the rest of the money or go more cheaply?" (No, you aren't allowed to just charge it and worry about paying for it later!)

Now, start throwing down ideas on paper. It doesn't matter how crazy they are. Make sure you write them down, because you will forget them as quickly as they come if you don't record them. Here are some off the top of my head:

1. You can use the frequent flyer miles and credit card bonus points you have been saving for years. You probably don't have enough to make it work, but you can use some of your Life Worth Assets and barter with someone who has them (you can bake cakes or paint someone's living room).

2. You can get a second job until you save up enough. Working at a kiosk at the mall on the weekends would probably get you enough money in a few months (you have Time on the weekends).

3. Maybe you can stay with someone out in Seattle who lives near the bay and save on hotel and food costs. (Life Worth Asset to be used: Social Currency. You will need to call around and find out if your cousin who used to live in Seattle has a friend who would welcome you).

4. Maybe you can "swap" houses with someone who lives in Seattle. If someone wants to come stay at your place for a week or two, use your car, and so forth, you can stay at their place. (You will need Knowledge about house

swapping. You can go online to get information about house swapping organizations and how to join).

5. Maybe you can work as a travel agent and organize a tour. If you get enough people committed to going, your airfare and hotel will be free or reduced. You can use your Social Currency. Not only do you have friends who can afford the trip, but they may have friends who want to go as well. You will need to increase your Knowledge so that you can give informational lectures on whales and their habits. You can also learn more about the Seattle area and arrange for sightseeing trips other than the whale watching tours. All this will take more Time. It means you probably will need to delay the trip a few weeks, but it will increase several Life Worth Assets. This could be the start of a series of trips.

6. Maybe you can combine the whale-watching trip with a business trip, so it would be partially tax deductible and save money.

7. Maybe you can go to a different location for whale watching that would be less expensive. Tours are also available on the East Coast of the US and Canada. If you have a friend who lives in a coastal city, maybe you can stay with her. Some places in South America might be cheaper, especially on the East Coast, and there are whale-watching excursions in the Caribbean. You can check into other possibilities. (This won't take much Time, and you certainly will be expanding your Knowledge. Maybe once you study about this, you can be more prepared to looking into #5, organizing a tour.)

8. Maybe a group could drive, or charter a bus, or maybe you have a friend who has a private plane would be willing to fly you there (That will take lots of Social Currency and, if you take a bus trip across country, Time).

9. If you go to the Caribbean, maybe you could find someone who owns a sailboat who would let you go if you pay the cost of using the boat, or in exchange for working on the boat. (Maybe your cooking skills will come in handy. You could fill in as the chef on a regular tour boat)

10. When your birthday/anniversary/Christmas comes up, you can request people make a contribution toward the trip instead of buying you a present.

You get the drift. It took me maybe 20 minutes to come up with these possible scenarios, and I haven't even begun to get rolling. Experts in Creative Thinking say that in order hatch up truly creative ideas, you have to concentrate on quantity, and not be concerned with quality. The first batch of ideas (the "first third") you envision generally are not very creative. They are the most predictable and the least likely to be truly exciting. Of course, if you may not want "exciting" ideas. For now, you just want to get in the water with the whales. But if you let yourself really dream, you might find yourself going into a direction that astonishes you and opens up avenues you never dreamed you would explore. Your soul could be stuffed with goodies!

Once you have exhausted the "sane" ideas, then the insane ones, the truly creative and innovative ideas will begin to emerge. That's the "second third." When you are tired and exhausted and your brain is screaming at you that there are no more possible ideas that could work is when you reach the "third third," the best and most innovative thoughts. Those are the ones that seem craziest at first, but if you tinker with them, they begin to show you a way to make something happen that is truly a grand idea. A third third idea might be: "We'll hitchhike to Seattle, camp out, and forage off the land."

Yes, that is crazy, but what can that crazy idea lead you to? How could you possibly safely hitchhike and camp out? Well. . . what if you found some way to get people interested in giving you a ride and places to stay and would sponsor your trip across country? Hmm. Who might do that? Who could you trust? How could you make it work?

Here's something: What if you contacted a national organization like the Save the Whales foundation and organized a fundraiser, where you and everyone you could recruit travel across the nation in order to raise awareness of the plight of the whales? You could arrange for supporters to pick you up in cars and buses and drive you across each state. You could stay in the homes of people who are willing to host you, people who have been properly vetted by the organization and who could offer safe housing. Maybe you could stay on college campuses, if you could get student organizations to back you. At the stopping place for each night, you would emcee a rally and fund drive for whale research and preservation. You could arrange for a whale-watching company out of Seattle to host the final event, and even organize a national-awareness day open to everyone.

Just a thought, one of many possible thoughts. If you arrange it right, it wouldn't cost a penny out of your pocket, and you would learn plenty about whales. You would become a champion for that magnificent mammal, and you would make lots of friends along the way. It would change your life, all because you were too broke to catch a plane to Seattle, but had the Drive, Creativity and Social Capital to work hard for your Dream. This might take much more Time than you had considered, but maybe it will change your life so much that the Time isn't an issue. It may lead you to a whole new career, a whole new Queendom. Don't laugh, it's happened before. People begin doing what they love, and the next thing you know, they've made a career of it.

Long term goal: Start a business photographing pets full time, and earn an income of at least $50,000 per year from it.

Sorry, you're on your own here. You'll need to come up with your own strategies since I don't know the first thing about any of that. You'd better get busy.

And then again, after you've arranged for that Save the Whales Caravan Across America, you might change your focus and exchange this long term goal for a different one. Maybe you'll photograph wild marine life instead.

You can work on several goals simultaneously as long as you focus on them regularly, ideally a little every day. By having a short term goal, you'll get some near-instant gratification, and that gives you courage to continue working on the others. Success breeds success, or rather it breeds Drive, which takes you to success. Once you have accomplished your first short term goal, you can pick up another one, but don't let short term goals keep you from working on the longer term ones as well.

It is possible that you have read this far without actually beginning the working process. But you will accomplish much more if you honor your Dreams enough to actually write them down. They are significant. They define you. They will mean far more to you and will do more for you if you pay attention to them rather than using this time to do the laundry or go grocery shopping. Eat PB & J tonight, let the laundry slide for a few days, pick up that pen and paper, and START WRITING DOWN YOUR DREAMS! Once you make the firm decision to do it, you're on your way. It will become more real to you, and since you will think through it and thoroughly understand what needs to be done, it will become more approachable and achievable.

Deborah Griffitts Hining

CHAPTER 8

SHOES

Pearls lie not on the seashore.
If thou desirest one thou must dive for it.

~Chinese Proverb

By listing your Strategies, you get a clear understanding of what really needs to be done in order to reach each Goal. To complete these Strategies, you need to think more specifically about what Actions you need to take. It's time to pay attention to the Horseshoes—those mundane bits of support for your Horses' feet, those day-to-day Actions that carry you forward to win your Queendom.

We are performing some Action every minute of every day of our lives. We choose, or fail to choose, the specific Action, but we always end up doing *something*. That something might be exactly what you should be doing to complete a Strategy, which in turn ultimately fulfills a Goal, or desire. And, of course, when you fulfill enough Goals, you achieve your Vision and build your Queendom. Or that something you happen to be doing at any given moment can be a pure waste of time—or worse, something that might actually make you lose ground.

At 6 pm today, you can be training for a marathon, like my former paraplanner Julie will be, or you can be watching NCIS reruns, like Mike and I often are. If I'm piled up on the couch rather than breaking in my hiking boots, I am getting even more out of shape than I was yesterday. It will be harder for me to limber up my knees and build my strength because I choose to veg out rather than work out. The Action or inaction we take is our choice, and what we choose to do from moment to moment really matters.

While I was in college, some of my friends tried some interesting drugs, messed themselves up or got busted, and dropped out. Some of those were drafted and sent to Viet Nam, and some of those were killed or maimed for life. A few got over it and went on to have healthy, contented lives. A few of my friends got pregnant after one too many margaritas. Some of those took subsequent Actions that turned out well, so that they went on to have happy lives; others took Actions that set them on a path of misery and heartbreak.

What we do or not do in any given moment can have very long and very large repercussions. Some of these repercussions may be out of proportion to the seeming insignificance of the Actions that led to them, and that may cause us to constantly be amazed at how unfair or beautifully serendipitous life can be. But if we remain aware that our Actions have consequences, we are much more likely to be thoughtful about the small decisions we make each minute. Our lives can pivot on a single Action. We are all smart enough to know that generally speaking, good choices lead us in a better direction than foolish ones do, and that if we want to accomplish something, we'd better get to work on it.

Penny Wisdom, Pound Genius

Taking it all in all, I find it is more trouble to watch after money than to get it.
~Michel Eyquem de Montaigne, 1572

Let's talk about money for a minute, just as an example of how small Actions can lead to large results. How you handle money from day to day, the thousands of decisions you make about how to save and spend it, have enormous implications over the course of your life. I have seen people get a sizeable windfall, blow it all within a few years, and end up practically destitute. It didn't seem like such a big deal to make a little celebratory trip, followed by a shopping spree. It was nice for them to quit being stingy with their children whose friends had all the new gadgets, and it was also nice to get a bunch of new gadgets for themselves. Each week, they bought a little something they would not have purchased if the windfall had not come along. Before anyone knew it, they had adopted spending patterns that they could not (or would not) stop.

I have seen people who decide to "invest" in property (aka a beach house they bought during the week of a fabulous vacation) by taking on a fat mortgage, with the happy idea they could rent it out to make the payments. But they failed to do the research to verify that, then found that there are far more properties on the beach for rent than there are renters to stay in them. They ended up with an asset that produces no income that they can't sell, and they can't keep up with the mortgage payments.

I have also seen people diligently save every month and forget that life is not about how much money one can store up. They ended up rich, but unhappy, and surprised by that fact.

Small, simple Actions regarding finances that require almost no time can make or ruin a decent life. One of my colleagues met with a new client whose husband had recently died. She was his second wife, and the couple had two children. Their life had been good for the eight years they had been married. He earned a very good living, and their children were smart, beautiful, and happy. But he was so busy plowing at his career, coaching soccer, and keeping their home in good repair that he failed to take care of one *tiny* little matter: He never changed the beneficiary on his life insurance and retirement plan at work, so his first wife remained the heir to nearly all his assets.

When he was killed in a boating accident at age 45, his family was suddenly thrown into terrible circumstances, because, believe it or not, his first wife was not inclined to share with her ex-husband's second family. Because he did not pay attention to his Horses' shoes, his wife and children were thrown into a life of struggle and hardship.

How you handle your money (and any of your Life Worth Assets) can have huge—enormous—*GIGANTIC* consequences: so much bigger than you can imagine. But let me help you. I'll just get out my calculator and limber up my fingers. Be prepared for a shock!

Let's say you are 22 years old, and you have just gotten your first real job. You are used to earning a student's income, but your new job now pays you $30,000, about $18,000 per year more than your last job did. What are you going to do with that extra money? Part of it will go to taxes, and assuming you didn't stupidly run up credit card debt while in school and you also don't have extra-hefty student loans, you have a lot of extra money that you didn't have before.

What Actions will you take regarding this money? You could do what most people do: immediately raise your standard of living by spending every dollar you bring home. You can get a new car, a nicer apartment, buy some new clothes, certainly some new shoes, and so on. And let's say you do just that. You feel that you deserve to have a little fun before you settle down and start that tedious old savings and investing stuff. So you wait until you start thinking about getting responsible at. . . oh, age 30 before you start investing into your company retirement savings plan. At that time, you start saving $300 per month.

Since you don't know anything about investing (your life is so busy, you really can't be bothered to learn about it), you put it in the only investment available that doesn't seem to be acting crazy, the fixed income fund, which has averaged 4.38% over time. You do that for the rest of your working life, never making changes, even though your income goes up regularly. You also never touch the money until you are ready to retire at age 62.

Do you know how much money you likely will have in 32 years? $246,200.

That's a nice chunk of change, but, sadly, not nearly enough to retire on. You've gotten used to living pretty high all those years you were earning a good income, and the money you saved will have to stretch out over all your entire retirement years. The bad news is you'll need to work for many more years before you have saved enough to replace your paycheck.

Let's back up and change just a couple of small things: Instead of waiting for those eight years between age 22 and 30 before you begin saving, you take a different Action. Rather than spending all of your new, fatter paychecks, you begin investing part of it, $300 per month (12% of your income) from the get-go. You also, at the age of 22, decide to be a bit more informed about how to invest your money, and you buy some books or engage a financial advisor who helps you understand that if you invest more aggressively and make the commitment to rebalance your portfolio to a proper mix just once each year, you may be able to assume a higher average rate of return over that 40 year period. Instead of a 4.38% rate, you might expect just over 9.01%, the average annual return of a moderately aggressive mix of

75% stocks, 25% bonds. Now, with these different assumptions, what is your ending pot of money likely to be worth?

You probably would expect it to be a little more than double, maybe even triple, because the rate of return is more than double, and you have an extra eight years of savings in the account. But the actual expected balance after 40 years on this portfolio would be about $1,295,000!

Gasp! You have increased your possible retirement pot by more than 5 times, simply because you began to consistently take some pretty easy Actions beginning at a young age. How difficult was that? How difficult will it be to spend that extra $million plus? If you find it too difficult, call me and I will help out.

Wait! Let's make some more tiny adjustments. Imagine that when you take your first job, you make the effort to seek out a position where your employer matches your savings plan contributions. Most larger companies, and many smaller ones do. A typical match rate is 50%, so if you contribute $300 per month, your employer contributes $150. Also, instead of investing a steady $300 per month from the beginning until you retire at 62, you make the commitment to increase your contributions each year as you get raises. Let's suppose your raises amount to 5% each year. In year one you make $30,000, and you invest $3,600. Your employer adds $1800. Year two you get a 5% raise to $31,500, and you invest $3,780, while your employer contributes $1,890. Each year your savings go up by 5%.

Maybe you won't make a 5% raise consistently every year, but I have found that most people do, over time, tend to increase their incomes by more than 5% per year on average as their careers progress. That's not much of a stretch. Let's also assume that you choose the more aggressive portfolio and take the trouble to rebalance every year. Now your probable ending balance at age 62?

Hold on to your hat! It's about to get exciting! At this rate of savings, with you and your employer increasing contributions by 5% each year and tending to your moderately aggressive portfolio carefully, your ending balance by the time you are 62 could be about $3,621,000! That's a difference of nearly $3,375,000 if you begin investing early, choose a moderately aggressive mix rather than a conservative one, get a company match, take the time to learn how to build and tend a portfolio, and increase your savings as you get raises over the years.

Three million, six hundred twenty one thousand dollars. If, at retirement, you invested that money in a moderately conservative mix returning about 7%, you could live on the income alone, without ever touching the principal for the rest of your life, with an income stream of income of $253,500 *per year.* That's a yearly income greater than the *total* amount you would have had in the first scenario. All this because you took certain small, deliberate Actions, such as gathering knowledge, hiring a competent professional, doing your research while searching for a job, and marching yourself down to the HR department the first week of your employment. Imagine the difference between $246,200 and $3,621,000 on your 62nd birthday. Forty years may seem like an awfully long time to do all this saving, but if you're diligent about it, chances are you can retire much earlier. Anyway, believe me, a decade or two or three goes by in a puff, and oh, that someone had taken me by the hand and explained all the above to me when I was a lass of 22!

Which Bag Goes Best With My Shoes?

Let's go back to your Goals and Dreams. Remember the short, medium and long term Goals we identified in the last chapter? Let's talk about the Strategies and Actions that will be necessary to accomplish some of them.

Short term goal: Join a soccer league

Of course the Strategy to reach that goal would be simple and easy—just sign up for one. But you can go for days, weeks, months, years, without actually joining that soccer league simply because you haven't gotten to the ACTION stage. In order to join that league, you actually have to pick up the phone and dial, or search out the website and log on. Then you have to get in the car and drive to the soccer field for every practice and game.

It isn't enough to say you're going to do it. You know you have to do it, but for some reason, you may find that actually taking the Action is much harder than dreaming about being a soccer star.

Why are we inclined to delay, or even fail to take the necessary Action to make something happen for our Queendom? Because we are lazy and stupid? No, I don't think so. I think it's partly because we are all somehow afraid that if we try to carry through, we might fail, or that it will take more Time and Energy than we are willing to commit. Also, as I pointed out in the last chapter, sometimes it's scary to think that we might actually *do* something extraordinary, which might mean that we might be required to *be* extraordinary!

Sometimes we just don't have enough Knowledge to know *what* to do, so we just let it slide. But mostly, I think we all are victims of inertia. It's hard to stop doing what we are doing (plowing in those ruts) and start doing something different.

Starting a new Action always is the hardest. Remember when you were in school and had to start a homework assignment and you really dreaded it? Writing that first paragraph was usually the toughest. Once you got started, it generally became easier to keep going. The decisions you make and Actions you take while plowing for your ordinary life are pretty easy. You are on autopilot there, and the constant repetitive Actions you make day after day gets you so in the groove that you find it almost effortless to keep it up. It's the new Actions that put you on a new path that take concentration and effort.

I met a young man recently who commented that he has big plans for himself, but he never gets around to doing anything to act on those plans because he has this big bag of excuses that he drags around with him. Whenever he thinks about doing something positive toward reaching his Dreams, he finds himself automatically reaching into his bag of excuses and pulling one out before he even has time to think about it.

"The fall semester starts in two months. I should sign up for that class I've been wanting to take. Oops, how did these excuses get into my hand? 'The class probably isn't offered this semester.' 'I probably won't have enough time to study.' 'I've heard that professor is really awful.' Oh, well. The deadline has passed. Guess I won't be taking the class this semester." And so he continues to live in his stale, unfulfilling life, unable or unwilling to take the Actions necessary to change it.

We all drag that enormous, floppy bag of excuses around with us. Heavy and awkward, it hangs around our neck and drags the ground. It's so much in the way we trip over it, and it catches on things so that it keeps us from going anywhere easily.

I've got a great idea! Let's burn that bag! Or at least let's plunk all the excuses spilling out of it over to the NOISE column and get them out of our lives. Now that you have a free hand, you can use it to reach into your other bag, the much more becoming (and practical) one, your bag of Life Worth Assets.

Reach into Your Bag of Life Worth Assets

Taking a look at the medium term goal from the last chapter, we need to figure out what Actions we should take to get it done, and what Life Worth Assets we have that can help.

Medium term goal: Take a whale watching canoe trip to the coast of Seattle

You have a number of Strategies that you have to complete by taking Actions. Of course, you have to talk to your friends and make arrangements, and so forth, but let's concentrate on the big issue that you need to deal with: Since you don't have enough Money to make it happen, you need to find a Strategy, using your other Life Worth Assets, to overcome the problem. We'll concentrate on one ones we explored in the last chapter.

Let's suppose you've decided you don't have enough Ambition & Drive, Creativity or Social Currency to choose the wild Strategy of organizing a March Across America to Save the Whales extravaganza. Rather, you just decided to work an extra job in order to earn the Money you need. What Actions must you get busy on? What Life Worth Assets to you have that will help you?

Are you willing to work at a second job in order to earn the Money? Do you have enough Time and Ambition & Drive to put in an extra 10-20 hours a week or so working? Do you want to take the trip badly enough so that you are willing to give up your nights and weekends? If not, maybe you need to move the whales over to the Noise side of your Vision and Dream list, or come up with alternate Strategies to make it happen. (And no, "Win the Lottery," or "Find a Sugar Daddy" probably are not the best Strategies).

But if you do have the Ambition & Drive to continue along the lines of earning extra Money, your first Action probably will be coming up with another Strategy: "Determine what I want to do to earn that money: work at a second job in retail, or start a sideline business, or something else."

Hmm, let's see. What are some of your Life Worth Skills that can earn you money? Are you a terrific cook? Maybe you could work in a restaurant on the weekends, or you could start a cake-baking business. Do you have a friend who is a docent at a high end art gallery who can get you a cushy, high paying job there? (Oh, my, that Social Currency does come in handy, doesn't it?) Do you love people and have an eye for fashion?

After all that examination, you may decide you are best suited to work retail at a high-end boutique:

Action 1. Tidy up your resume (Use your Life Worth Asset of good writing skills, or dig into your Social Currency purse and get someone to help you.)

Action 2. Go around to different stores to see if any openings are available. Ask your friends!

Action 3. Read the Want Ads, check out Craig's List, and other possible Help Wanted outlets.

Action 4. Make sure you have the right clothes and "look" to make an impression on boutique owners and managers. (Don't go into debt to buy new clothes! Make do with a few new accessories. You might borrow some clothes from a friend.)

Action 5. Contact stores, fill out applications, go to interviews.

Action 6. Take the job, work consistently.

Action 7. Save the Money until you have enough.

Of course, you have many other Strategies that need to be taken care of before you make it to Seattle and into that canoe, but if you consistently drive your Actions toward completing the Strategies, you WILL get there, no matter how big the Dream.

Act Now Before You Grow a Day Older!

As you begin to determine what Strategies you will choose to get you off to the Whale Watch, you may find that your Dreams, and even your Vision will change. What started out as "wouldn't it be nice to go see the whales," could turn into "I want to do what I can to preserve and protect the whales around the globe," or, "I have discovered I really love working retail in the high-end fashion industry." That might lead you making life-changing decisions—all because you began to really look at your desires and determine what your life should look like. You can dream up a Queendom and build it Action by Action, Horseshoe by Horseshoe.

You will have many Actions to complete before you can actually make that trip or change your career, and the more ambitious the Dream, the longer the list of Actions that will have to be accomplished. As you work on your list, you will think about how important every little Action or inaction can be when it comes to taking charge of your Queendom.

The fact remains that if we *don't* do the things on the list, guess what? You won't get in the boat next to those whales, and I won't make it to the mountains to hike this summer, and our souls will starve yet another few months or years. When a soul is not fed it shrinks and pines, and then begins to demand shopping trips to fill the hollow spaces.

The fact is, your future is what you make it. Sure, life will throw you curves that you won't see coming, and your future will never be exactly as you envision it. But your moment-to-moment reality, the life, or the Queendom, that you are actually living, is almost entirely up to you, the decisions you make, the Strategies you develop, and the Actions that you follow through with. And the future that follows will spring out of that moment-to-moment reality. It is never set in stone. You may be on one track now, but the smallest changes can set you on a new trajectory that veers your path into an entirely new direction. That new direction may be perfect, and you may decide to stay on it. Or you might need to change your course of direction to put yourself back onto the right path.

If you haven't already done so, take the time to complete that little chore of writing down all the Actions you need to take to complete the Strategies that will allow you to reach your Goals so you can define your Vision so that you can build and live well in your Queendom.

If you choose to actually do everything on each and every list, without dragging your feet, your Queendom will materialize as surely as tulips bloom in April. If you make that phone call, set that appointment, clear your schedule, go to the gym, and make sure you complete every task that you set down, you *will* create the reality you want. Think of it as plowing for your Queendom, and to do it, you have to make sure those horses are well shod.

CHAPTER 9

NAILS

All that we are is the result of what we have thought
~Buddha

This chapter might have come first. Ben Franklin would have agreed that if you have no way to attach Horseshoes to your Horses, your whole Queendom could be lost, so in a way, absolutely everything important in your life hinges on those little bitty Nails. The Nails you need in your Queendom are weightless, but sharp, and strong as steel. They are your very Thoughts, and like the nails that are hammered into horses' hoofs, they must be well shaped, tempered, and honed. If they are bent or soft or missing entirely, your Horses can't function, hobbling around on tender feet. Building and defending a Queendom requires a sharp, powerful thinking process.

I know you have been thinking hard as you have worked to define your Vision and build your Queendom, but I bet at times it has been difficult to focus completely on the task and to keep your Thoughts organized. Even though we are always thinking about *something*, most of the time, our brains are not fully engaged with any one thing. When you drove in to work this morning, you probably didn't use much of your brain to drive (the guy in front of me certainly didn't!), and so most likely your Thoughts strolled around, glancing here and there at other things: what your husband said last night, the phone calls you had to return, how much you would enjoy being an Olympic champion . . . The brain loves to laze around and dabble in many things at once.

Deborah Griffitts Hining

Why Do We Think the Thoughts We Think?

Let's face it. Most of us do not use our brains as effectively as we could, and rarely do we take full charge of our Thoughts. It's a myth that we use only about 10% of our brain capacity, but what we do use is pretty undisciplined. We let our minds run amok, and only occasionally, when we are under a tight deadline or when we are trying to formulate a compelling argument or a new theory, do we summon up the focus it takes to be really productive.

It sure would be nice if we could get things under control and consistently be able to think only the Thoughts we wanted to think. Right now I would like to be thinking about the next sentence I am going to write, but other Thoughts keep popping up to obstruct my clarity and purpose. If I write with a pure stream of consciousness, it would probably go like this:

Your Thoughts are. . . Boy! It's a nice day! I wonder if those asters will come back this year. Of course, they don't bloom 'til autumn. . . It will be autumn in Australia soon. . . Is that where lemmings come from? Why on earth do they commit suicide like that?. . .Where was I? Oh yes, Your Thoughts are. . . wonder how long it would take me to learn to play the piano?

Naturally, it hasn't been easy to keep my Thoughts going in the direction I want them to go, for it seems that my brain has a mind of its own, so to speak. It's not that I'm particularly mindless. It's just that my Thoughts are influenced by far more than I would like them to be. Here are some of the forces that cause us to think like we do:

Past Experiences

The school of hard knocks is
an accelerated curriculum
~Menander of Athens (Ancient Greek poet)

Every experience teaches us something, and as we learn, our brain stores the memory, recalling it not only whenever a similar experience or situation arises, but also often in very different contexts. The more often experiences are repeated, the more we solidify the thought processes that have been connected to it. As these thought patterns are consistently reinforced, the brain actually changes physically. New synapses form and strengthen, and eventually, our Thoughts become so solidified that it becomes difficult, perhaps even impossible to think differently.

Imagine a rivulet that is formed during a rainstorm. Each time another rainstorm comes along, the rivulet deepens and becomes wider. Eventually, a creek or river develops where only a trickle used to be. While a rivulet might easily be diverted, diverting a deep river becomes much more difficult. As we get up every morning, pick up that plow, and think the same old thoughts, it isn't our plows that form the entrenched, boring furrows: it's our minds.

When thought processes have become deeply established, we find it very difficult to break out of those patterns, even if our situation has changed, or even if we are aware that a change in Thought or expectation can change our lives for the better. This disinclination to think differently, or "confirmation bias," as they call it in psychologist-speak, sends deep roots into our psyche that dictate who we are and what we think. It is hard to circumvent, because once we believe that something is true, both our conscious and subconscious minds continually look for ways to confirm it.[1]

Deborah Griffitts Hining

If you've had your heart broken by a conniving man, you might be able to get over it and come to trust another man at another time. If the new guy treats you badly, it won't be so easy to trust again. After the third and fourth times it happens, you might just decide that all men are shits, and you are done with them. You have formed a confirmation bias, and even if a wonderful man comes along who treats you with nothing but kindness and love, it may take a very, very long time to learn to trust him. It will take conscious work, and perhaps even the aid of a therapist for you to get over your deep-seated distrust.

Redirecting your thought processes so that you come to different conclusions about any kind of situation takes deliberate, intense work, similar to what it takes to learn any new skill or behavior, like learning to play the saxophone. Every time you practice, your brain is modified. New synapses form and new neurons are laid down. After weeks and months of practice, your brain becomes accustomed to the fingering and rhythmic patterns required to play, so that eventually you can pick that baby up and wail away with great skill.

In the same way, you can change the thought processes you are accustomed to in any life situation. You don't have to be what you have always been. You don't have to think the way you have always thought. You can start by choosing to change your confirmation bias.

If you want to win the battle for your beautiful Queendom, you have to start by thinking about it. First, you have to decide to do it, and then discipline yourself to think carefully through every step of the process. You also should learn to recognize when you are starting to think in a way that is contrary to your Vision. Each time you find yourself thinking in ways that contradict or thwart your deep values and desires, you can get back on track by deliberately choosing to think something more constructive.

Let's say you have an acquaintance who sometimes says snide things to you. She does it so often that every time she talks to you, you have come to expect that she is going to give you a backhanded compliment that really is an insult. Before long, you find that she insults you every time you talk to her. She may say, "That's an interesting dress you're wearing," but you, in your programmed brain, hear, "horrible dress." In reality, her intent may not be to insult you, but because of past experience, you certainly hear that. This, of course, makes you angry and unhappy.

Is that thought process a good thing for you? Does it help you fulfill your Vision for yourself? Does it help you to reach some of the Goals you set for yourself? Likely not. Now, here's the trick to taking charge of your life and guarding your Queendom against that traitorous Noise that comes at us so often: The next time she says something that you perceive as hurtful, you must remember that her words have not hurt you. You are hurt only because *you have chosen* to be hurt. Never mind what she meant. *You* chose to interpret her comment in the worst possible light, and *you* chose to react in a negative way.

In reality, you have much more control over the situation than you might have believed. It's just possible that she is unaware that she is being hurtful to you, or perhaps she perceives you as her enemy because in the past you did something that she chose to interpret negatively, and she saw it as a declaration of war. Who knows who was the first to pick up the stick and draw the battle lines? Your confirmation bias against her may have been formed under mistaken circumstances, just as hers is against you.

The next time you meet this person, try changing your thought processes by interpreting everything she says in the *best* possible light. If she says, "interesting dress," try telling yourself that she particularly likes anything "interesting." After all, you did buy it because it was different from everything else you see at the chain stores. You have the choice to interpret her comment in any way you wish, and how you interpret any experience determines how you are going to feel about it.

If it's impossible to put a positive spin on what she says without warping reality beyond reason, you can choose to interpret her sourness on the fact that she may be having a bad day or that she is sad or depressed with her own life, and she needs someone to be kind to her. If you repeatedly change the dynamics of the conversation by selecting what you choose to think and say, you eventually may be able to change your relationship with her. She may not become your BFF overnight, but even if she never changes her attitude toward you, you can change your reaction—and your feelings—toward her. Life is too short and your Queendom is too precious to let bad experiences darken it. Cut everybody as much slack as you can. It will lighten your own load.

Current Circumstances

Do not let circumstances influence your thoughts and moods. By rising over them mentally, you will eventually rise over them materially.

~Remez Sasson (writer)

Just as experiences form and modify your Thoughts and feelings, any circumstance that you are in at any given time has a great deal of influence over your Thoughts and your mood. The human mind tends to believe that whatever circumstances it is experiencing at this moment will continue forever, no matter how much we may "know better."

Spring always follows winter, but deep in the darkness of January, we sometimes think that the sun will never shine again and tulips will never bloom. In the long, hot days of summer, it's hard to believe that it's freezing cold in other parts of the world. I spent a very shivery summer in Scotland once. When I was packing in 95 degree heat, I just couldn't bring myself to pack anything heavier than one light sweater alongside my sleeveless tank tops, light skirts, and sandals. Although I was warned that it could be cold there in June and July, I couldn't believe that I would actually need layers of woolen clothing. My present circumstances ruled my Thoughts and made my visit to Scotland uncomfortable.

During the boom years of the late '90s, my clients always left my office in a good mood. They were happy that their investment accounts were growing fat and that they were ahead of pace for retirement. They were able to buy the new car they wanted or take the longed-for trip a little earlier than they had planned. They began to get a little cocky about their ability to tolerate volatility, and some decided that they were really very aggressive investors. As a matter of fact, they began to love volatility, because upside volatility was very easy to take.

Talking people into keeping their portfolios balanced by selling off some of the excess stock to buy bonds was very difficult during these times. Why, they asked, would they want to get the measly 5-7% return that bonds average when it was easy to get ten times that in equities? Fed chairman Greenspan saw the precipitous rise in stock prices and chastised people for their "irrational exuberance," warning them to stop driving up the stock market, but nobody wanted to listen to the doomsayers. Everyone preferred the reports by the analysts who believed that the stock market would continue to rise well into the 21st century. It didn't. Instead, it collapsed early in 2000.

In 2000, 2001, and 2002, I handed out a lot of Kleenex, and I also had to remind people that the stock market would eventually recover, and that it is better to buy than to sell when prices are low. Still, some begged to move their dwindling stock accounts over to cash in order to "stop the bleeding." According to them, the market was going to continue to plummet until their accounts were worth exactly $0, and they would have to work until they were at least 100 years old or dead, whichever came first. They completely forgot the halcyon days of just a few years earlier.

Then came the recovery of 2003-2007. Suddenly, making money was easy again, and everyone found that their risk tolerance was getting a little higher—or much higher. Good times were here and they were here to stay this time—that is, until the most recent crash in 2008! The economy then entered a horrible period that would no doubt continue for the next 40 or 50 or 100 years.

Then, when 2011 rolled around, people were wishing they had listened to me when I told them to buy stocks early in 2009 when they were very cheap. But hey, now that the market is charging back up, they'd like to get into something really hot, please.

The human mind is far less rational than we would like to believe it is, and immediate circumstances can influence our thought processes much more than we realize. Be careful not to let mob psychology or current conditions sway your decision-making. Rather, let your decisions and Thoughts help you to change your circumstances. Eventually, the tide will turn. The person who stays calm in the face of frenzy is much better off than the person who gets caught up in it.

However, remember to stay flexible. Sometimes a surprising new circumstance will pop up fortuitously. If you have your eyes on your Vision, you may be able to see how this new event can lead you straight to your Queendom. You control your circumstances partly by knowing which circumstances to take advantage of because they take you down the right path and which   to ignore because they lead you off into the wilderness!

Gender

If a woman has to choose between catching a fly ball and saving an infant's life, she will choose to save the infant's life without even considering if there are men on base.

~Dave Barry

Just being female predisposes us to think certain ways. It is well established that men's and women's brains are structured differently. The right hemisphere, where logical thought and speech functions take place, tends to be larger in men's brains, but women tend to have greater mass in the left hemisphere where the communication center lies.

There is a big difference in the size and number of emotional centers as well. Men have two emotional centers, both of which are located in the right hemisphere. Brain scans reveal that their emotional centers become active in an emotional situation, as you would expect.

We women, however, have an embarrassment of emotional riches in our brains: we have *nine* emotional centers, located throughout the whole brain, and they are active virtually *all the time*! Dr. Brizendine sums up the difference in her book, *The Female Brain*: "Women have an eight–lane superhighway for processing emotion, while men have a small country road."[2] Between the more robust communication and emotional centers, women are more inclined to think about relationships, emotions, and the needs of other people.[3]

Men, as your mother told you, tend to think more about power and sex. According to Brizendine: they "have larger brain centers for action and aggression, and two and a half times the brain space devoted to sexual drive." She makes an eloquent comparison: They "have O'Hare Airport as a hub for processing thoughts about sex, where women have the airfield nearby that lands small and private planes."[4] Just thought you might like to have that cleared up once and for all.

If you consider that everything that goes on inside your head as Thought, then a woman's brain is a busy place indeed. Our brains work like computers, or several people working together on one chore. Both brain hemispheres chatter away to each other, using several centers simultaneously, no matter what the subject matter is. Our minds move with lightening speed from point A to point C and B, then back to emotion D and then revisiting point A again because emotion D shed a different light on the matter. And then—oh wait!—here is a new bit of information about the social implications of a possible decision, which makes us revisit the whole picture again. So that's A,C,B,D, A,E,A,C,B,D,A in a flash. And what does that do for us? It keeps the mint for Social Currency operating at full tilt.

Men's brains aren't quite so active. They tend to use only one hemisphere at a time, and their processing capabilities are linear, like an adding machine or a person walking from point to point. They deliberate along a straight line: A. ....B.... C. *Decision made. Don't bother me with any new, irrelevant emotional considerations.*[5] They like to believe this makes them more "logical," and brag that they make more sense than we do. That's ok, we like to indulge their cute little notions—they're just so adorable when they strut around, aren't they?

Chemistry

Never underestimate the power of estrogen
~Anonymous

If the female brain's structure provides the foundation for empathetic, nurturing thinking, regular hormone surges nudge us even further into thought patterns, which reinforce social connection. Our need for oxytocin, the feel-good "bonding" hormone makes us far more likely than men to think about the needs and desires of others.

Other chemicals and hormones influence our Thoughts as well. If you've ever noticed that you tend to think nicer Thoughts around the middle of the month, and nasty ones while in the throes of PMS, you've been aware of how chemistry affects your thought processes. Alcohol and mind altering drugs can radically alter your Thoughts. People who are clinically insane can be effectively treated with drugs to combat chemical imbalances in the brain. Even depression which causes people to obsess about suicide can be alleviated by the right drug therapy.

Emotions influence Thought and attitude so much because the hormones that are triggered with each emotion can be so powerful. When you are depressed, your Thoughts—and your body chemistry—are quite different than when you are happy. Ordinarily, you might like hugs from a friend, but if you're having a crappy day, you might want to snap at someone who tries to hug you. On the other hand, if you've just won the lottery, you might happily welcome the embrace of your creepy neighbor you've never liked the smell of.

Not only does the chemical balance associated with emotions have a powerful influence on Thought and behavior, but the relationship between the two also works the other way around. You can change your brain chemistry, and your mood, not only with hormones and drugs, but also by changing your behavior and your Thoughts, just as you can change the physical structure of your brain with behavior and conscious Thought. What we do in a given situation actually creates our mood and alters our thought processes.

Let's go back to the situation with your catty friend. Whenever you lay eyes on her, your oxytocin and serotonin levels are likely to plummet, and you may immediately start thinking very unhappy Thoughts. If she says something you perceive as mean, you may go so far as to believe that she hates you and is out to get you. This will lower your serotonin even further, depressing you and causing you to think even more negatively. But if you find a reason to be upbeat—say you tell yourself that the reason she is unkind is because she is having a bad day, or she believes you dislike her because you inadvertently hurt her feelings once, and that she really would like to mend the relationship, your serotonin level will rise, and you are likely to think more positive Thoughts and to feel better about yourself and about her.[6]

Associates and Associations

Bad company corrupts good character
~Menander of Athens

You have heard it said that you are what you eat. It is more likely that you are what you immerse yourself into: what you read; what you watch on TV; what you look at on the Internet; the people with whom you associate. Whatever we spend our time with absorbs into our brains and literally restructures them. Read an uplifting book, and you feel uplifted; your Thoughts become more positive, creative, tolerant, and serene. Feed yourself a steady diet of angry, depressed movies and books, and your brain becomes a morass of murky swamp water hiding who-knows-what kind of horrid creatures. You can't help it. What you put into your brain is going to rewire it so that it becomes the focus of your Thoughts.

The more time we spend with any one type of people, the more likely we are to start thinking like those people. Hang out exclusively with a bunch of catty bitches, and the next thing you know, you've become one yourself. Constantly be in the presence of political activists who believe in pushing the envelope, and before long, you may be thinking radical, even anarchist Thoughts. Enjoy the company of Mary Poppins, and your life becomes a Broadway musical.

Back in Chapter 4, I discussed briefly how we shouldn't restrict our relationships to people who make us feel good, but we should also be true friends to all kinds of people, even the ones we might consider negative. Let's explore that a bit more.

The world breaks down into two essential types of people: optimists and pessimists. Optimists are happy thinkers: They see the good in everything and in everyone. They believe that, no matter how bad the circumstances, everything will always work out fine in the end, that ultimately, the universe is a friendly place. They have great ideas, all of which have promise and hope. It's nice to be an optimistic thinker, and to have lots of optimistic friends. Fall into a nest of optimists, and life is just a bowl of cherries. If you tend toward the pessimistic side, be sure you surround yourself with optimists, and let some of their enthusiasm rub off on you. You can't help but feel better and become more creative.

An optimist sees nothing but possibilities. She can walk into a derelict house, full of snakes and rotten floors, and see only the beautiful crown moldings, the 12 foot ceilings, the magnificent sweep of the staircase. She wants to buy it immediately and restore it, because she sees only the vision of a resplendent mansion. Nowhere in her head is any idea of the backbreaking work, the late nights scrubbing and scraping, the heartbreaking setbacks, the monumental expense of renovations. And therein lies the downside to perpetually optimistic thinking. It can lead you down a garden path that may not necessarily end in that bowl of cherries. It flat-out can get you into trouble.

I have had the mixed blessing of being born an untempered optimist. When I was seven years old, I thought it would be fun to turn a cartwheel while jumping rope. After all, I could practically fly, so a cartwheel would be nothing. Today, I am walking around without all of my own front teeth. When I was 10 years old, I decided it was time to learn to swim. The best way to do that, of course, would be to jump off the dock into the lake. My body, in a fit of self-preservation would no doubt immediately rise to the challenge, and then I would miraculously become a class-A swimmer. I never got around to thanking the old man who noticed me floundering and glub-glubbing, and pulled me out just as I went down for the third time. I have bought my share of beautiful houses even though my architect husband gently pointed out the crumbling foundations and walls full of black mold ("Come on, you can fix it," I wheedle. Fortunately, he's an optimist, too),

Thank goodness I have learned to cultivate a bit of a pessimistic streak over the years. Consequently, I still have most of my teeth, and I haven't come close to drowning in a very long time. I now tend to think things through before I rush off half-cocked, and whenever one of my clients enthusiastically informs me she has found a gorgeous property on the beach that she can sink her life savings into ("only needs a bit of restoration!"), I am able to convincingly point out the downsides.

Yes, you are generally happier if you always think positive Thoughts, and you should have as many optimistic friends as you can find. However, if you are too much of an optimist, you should learn to develop some pessimistic thinking as well, and you certainly should cultivate at least a few friends that our culture today would disdainfully call "negative." The more variety you have in your friends, the more your own mind will expand, and the more you will be able to look at the world in an open, accepting way. But when you are searching out those pessimists, be careful. There are the good ones, but there are also the bad ones, and there certainly are the ugly ones. You can have all you want of the good, try to be sparing with the bad, but when you encounter an ugly, quickly tiptoe backwards out of the room before he notices you.

The Good

Good pessimists tend to dwell on negative things, but they try not to inflict their negativity upon their friends. Knowing how irritating they can be, they tend to keep their negative opinions mostly to themselves, at least until they see some glaring pending disasters. Then they have the wonderful knack of gently pointing out all the bad things that could possibly happen. By doing so, they take that necessary burden away from your shoulders. These friends, called "defensive pessimists" by psychologist Julie K, Norem, PhD[7], can take a seemingly wonderful idea and immediately zero in on every flaw in the Goals and Strategies you have dreamed up to build your Queendom.

But the thing that most makes these pessimists "good" is the fact that they don't say the Goals or Strategies can't be accomplished, and they don't tell you your Vision is silly. They simply point out the things that might foul up the works, and so help you understand what needs to be done to ensure success. Defensive pessimists are a great foil to unbridled optimists. You need both on your team so that you can develop better Strategies to build your Queendom with the fewest numbers of upsets.

The Bad

These people aren't really bad, they're just hopelessly negative. They are the miserable Eyores who simply give up or start muttering discouraging comments before you even can flesh out the Vision you may be cooking up. They see the universe as an unfriendly place.

Let's say you have decided to organize that Save The Whales Trip Across America. A good pessimist will remind you that you need to ensure the safety of the group. She will come up with specific problems you may encounter: "There is a good likelihood that some real weirdoes will volunteer to put up the 19 year old girls in his extra bedroom for the night." That never would occur to an optimist, of course, but such a Thought will come to a good pessimist right from the beginning. That, and the fact that there will be flat tires and 100 degree heat and very few people willing to drive you across the badlands and some really stinky sleeping accommodations along the way, and etc., etc., etc. A defensive pessimist may not be much fun when she's rattling off the possible disasters, but she sure can alert you to what needs to be taken care of before the trip.

A bad pessimist, however, will simply say, "That's impossible." If you ask why, she will respond with vague reasons. "It's not safe. You can't get enough people to help out. It's too much work." Bad pessimists are slippery. They know bad things can happen, but you can't pin them down enough to identify those bad things. There is no way to argue because there is no real issue to argue about. It just is.

Bad pessimists aren't necessarily poisonous to your Queendom. Their thought processes are harder to deal with, and they are likely to be huge wet blankets, but they can teach you to think through your Strategies more completely. Because they are vague, they can force *you* to sharpen your own Thoughts and be specific about potential problems. They can teach you to protect your own Vision. If you are an optimist, bad pessimists are your cross to bear. You have enough goodwill to go around, so take the effort to encourage them. If you, yourself, are a bad pessimist, you'd better go looking for some wildly exuberant optimists to befriend. You'll need them. And for heaven's sake, read the upcoming section on Creativity very closely!

The Ugly

Sigh. I really didn't want to have to talk about this, but it's a sad fact of life that there are truly ugly people in the world. If they are pessimistic, it isn't because they are really worried about the way things might turn out for you, but simply because they don't want you to succeed. They may even wish to do you harm. My talented beauty queen student I mentioned in Chapter 4 was hamstrung by an ugly pessimist who claimed to be her friend. Don't hang out with people who are inherently mean and spiteful and who look for ways to hurt others. You don't want to be their victim, and you certainly don't want to become one. They will poison your Thoughts in about the same length of time it took Scarlett O'Hara to steal Frank Kennedy from her sister Suellen.

By the way, going back to that catty friend who constantly insults you: If, after you have really tried to change your relationship and fail, get away from her. She probably is an Ugly. It's a big world, and you can build your good Queendom far away from her hellish one.

Exercise

Our minds are lazier than our bodies.
~François, Duc de La Rochefoucauld,
Maxims, 1678

Scientists are just now discovering how remarkable the brain really is. "The mature brain is extraordinarily plastic," says David Amaral, a neuroanatomist at the University of California, Davis. "Dendrites are growing and retracting, synapse are falling apart—there's a lot more potential for growth and change than we used to realize."[8]

The brain is just like a muscle: the more stretching and heavy lifting you do with it, the stronger and more flexible it becomes. If challenged, it learns that there are alternate ways of thinking that might be more appropriate and beneficial than the ways it might have been thinking in the past. One of the best ways to exercise the brain is by education. Studying any subject diligently causes it to grow and become more robust. Back when I was studying Renaissance literature, I could feel my brain growing quicker and expanding in new areas, and after just a few classes, I could pick up something as esoteric as Shakespeare's *King Lear* and read it effortlessly and with great pleasure. I could appreciate the parallel construction of the language, the imagery, and the cultural context. I might say something like, "Oh, that's interesting. In this passage, Lear refers to his daughters as pelicans. That's a very clear image, since in those days, people thought that pelicans ripped open their own breasts and let their offspring feed on their blood. It also implies the extent of pain they are causing him."

I haven't read Shakespeare in decades (these days I lean more toward what you might call "light reading"), and now that my brain has gone soft and flabby, I can feel it getting winded if I try to absorb anything more dense than *People Magazine*. (You can imagine what an effort it is to write this chapter. I have to take a nap after each section!) If today, I should pick up a copy of *Lear* and read a line, "The prince of darkness is a gentleman: Modo he's call'd, and Mahu," my brain goes: "Huh? Whuzzat mean? Man, I'm tired! Wonder what's on TV?"

Think Better

When you have control over your thoughts,
you have control over your life.

~Remez Sasson

Thinking is the most important thing we can do, because we eventually became what we think about. Whatever we dwell upon most dictates the direction we take. We blaze our life path with Thought, and we pave it with Action.

Experts in productive thinking processes, philosophers, and creative geniuses agree that we all would be better off if we learned to think better and to use our brains more productively. If we don't consciously learn to think critically and to think for ourselves, we become slaves to the whims and machinations of others (see Chapter 2) and to the unproductive ruts we find ourselves in. As Notre Dame philosophy professor Tom Morris writes:

We need time to think. Some time to reflect on who we are, where we are, what we are doing, and what we enjoy, what we value, what we love, and what we really want to accomplish. We need time to ask ourselves some questions and time to formulate some answers. . .[9] We are no longer accustomed to articulating and clarifying our thoughts, our beliefs, our hopes, and our goals on a regular basis. So much in contemporary culture seems to militate against this. We're in such a hurry. We are too busy. We're on the go. We obviously have some bad habits, habits of inarticulateness about who we are and what we really want out of life, patterns of neglect that urgently need to be changed.[10]

If we can learn to think better, we will achieve our Queendoms much more effectively than if we let circumstances, other people, and the ruts in front of us dictate our minds' activities. Good thinking skills give us several advantages:

First, insightful Thought allows us to weed through all the Noise so that we can understand ourselves and what we really want;

Second, clarifying our Vision takes us through a process that allows us to fully understand *why* we want to do what we want to do. It helps to solidify our values;

Third, understanding how our desires reinforce our deeply held values seats our Vision well enough into our brains and hearts so that we gain enough Drive to actively work toward achieving our Queendoms; and

Fourth, thinking well helps us to actually build our Queendoms just the way we want them to be. Trying to go about it willy-nilly, making a stab at it every now and then doesn't work very well. It takes focused effort to construct the blueprints and commit to the Actions it takes to build it stone by stone. Directing and focusing your mental energies helps you build your Queendom by keeping a positive, creative attitude alive, and gets you organized well enough to complete the tasks necessary to carry forward.

CREATIVE VS PRACTICAL THINKING

Necessary Tools:
*Pen and paper, optimist's hat and
pessimist's hat, cards of Goals*

Truly productive thinking, the kind required to dream up and build your Queendom, is made up of two distinctive mental skills, creative thinking and critical thinking. Creative, or possibility thinking is more fun; it's all about dreaming. Practical thinking is much easier for anyone but the most unbridled of optimists. It requires you to think

Deborah Griffitts Hining

about all the bad things that can happen to ruin your plans. Creative thinking is actually a bit harder to master than critical thinking is because our Western schooling has tended to emphasize critical thinking. Most people can think creatively, but we tend to take it less seriously, and we usually switch over to critical thinking prematurely, before we have allowed our creative Thoughts to fully flower.

As you build your Queendom, you will need to have two hats: A creative thinking, or optimist's hat, and a critical thinking, or pessimist's hat. Your creative thinking hat might be a big, blue or yellow hat with a few peacock feathers in it, and several green, red, and purple ribbons tied into it. It may have some glitter and sequins on it as well grapes and a pineapple. Oh, and some illusion. Definitely some gossamer illusion. If you don't already have such a hat, spend some time constructing one, at least in your mind. You simply cannot be less than wildly creative while wearing this wonder.

Your critical thinking, or pessimist's hat is quite different. This hat, while not at all ugly, is quite prim. It may be a nice, trim little beret, or a Jackie-type pillbox with a birdcage veil. Maybe an understated sun hat trimmed with no more than some little pleated ribbons around the brim. But it is definitely nothing like your creative hat. This is one you wouldn't mind wearing in public.

Now, keep in mind that you cannot wear both hats at once. When you are wearing your optimist's hat, you are allowed to think creative thoughts, and creative thoughts *only*. Before you can allow yourself to start thinking negatively, pessimistically, or critically, you must make the deliberate step of taking off your optimist's hat and putting on the other. When you are wearing your pessimist's hat, you must think critical thoughts *only*. This will help you give each type of thinking its due so that you don't diminish the brilliance of your ideas or shortchange the seriousness of problems that need to be thought through. Are you ready? Now, we're picking up that pen again.

Creative Thinking

Let's go back to Chapter 6 and look at the dreaming exercises again. Pick a Goal that is a little crazy, but not absolutely impossible to achieve. How about: Take a year off work and go live in Paris. Put on your gaudy, glitzy, gauzy hat and start thinking and writing.

What wonderful things can you imagine about living in Paris? Do you see sidewalk cafes and summer breezes and long walks through glistening streets littered with cherry blossoms? Artists and interesting people and wine and trips to Mont St. Michele, Versailles, and Giverny? Long afternoons in the Louvre and boat rides on the Seine, and oh, my goodness, maybe a romance and new friends. . . .

And then there are the longer term benefits. By spending time in Paris, you would improve your French, expand your horizons, maybe make some interesting and helpful connections. Maybe it will open up whole new directions for your life that you haven't even begun to dream about. Keep thinking. What will you do while you are there? Who will you meet? Will you fall in love? Will you become fluent in French? Will you discover a new career? Will you live in a wonderful little apartment with a balcony overlooking the Seine? Will you start your novel? Will you begin designing your new line of clothing? What is impossible, but wonderful to imagine? How about you become a painter as great as Monet? Or Louis Vuitton asks you to design a new handbag for their line? The possibilities are dizzying! What would you really like to see happen?

Creative thinking is expansive, generative, and non-judgmental. Of course, it requires Imagination, and plenty of it. While you are generating ideas for how you want your Queendom to look, you need to keep your Thoughts confined to imagining only the positive, and don't reject any Thoughts simply because they might seem silly or unachievable or outlandish. Believe that every idea you have is wonderful and do not allow any doubts about any of them to creep in when you are brainstorming.

Creative thinking is elusive. It's very difficult to come up with completely new ideas, and takes a lot of free-wheeling brainstorming to get to the truly creative stage. Let me remind you that experts in creative thinking insist that you must come up with huge quantities of ideas while you are brainstorming, because the first ideas you come up with aren't new ideas at all. They simply are regurgitations of old ones you were already aware of.[12] You need to push to break through the staid, and into the truly fresh ideas.

Creative thinking also is ephemeral. Once you get going, ideas will flit through your head and out into the ether quickly. You may find that ideas come to you in the middle of the night or while you are brushing your teeth, and if you don't write them down immediately, you will not be able to remember them. I think I may have mentioned this a time or two already. Have you started listing your Dreams yet? Do you have a pen in your hand right now?

Practical Thinking

Once you have exhausted all possible wonderful reasons why you should go live in Paris for a year, it's time to change hats. Deliberately take off your optimist's hat and put on your pessimist's hat. Turn your Thoughts away from the giddy heights of dreaming and start imagining all the things that could possibly spoil your plans. As any good pessimist will tell you, it's vital to imagine the negatives so you can be prepared to battle all the possible dangers that may be facing you.

Begin your list. What could possibly happen to spoil your Paris adventure? For starters, you could fall off the Eiffel tower and die in a foreign country where there is no one to claim your body and bury you. You could be run over by a taxi, you could fall into the Seine and drown. You could be kidnapped by a gang of human traffickers and sent off to some horrible corner of the world to work in coal mines, and never see the light of day again. You could be arrested on some trumped-up charge and chained to the wall in a medieval dungeon and eaten by rats.

I know those fears might not be legitimate. But go ahead and let your imagination run wild and write down all the crazy possibilities because, let's face it, you might actually have some of those really wild Thoughts lurking around vaguely in the muddy depths of your mind. Rather than allowing yourself to fear generally and vaguely, clarify, examine, and articulate every possible fear.

Of course there also will be legitimate concerns. Here is one: What if you run out of money? Examine this one closely, and be as specific as you can about what could happen to cause you to run out of money. Here are just a few:

What if the exchange rate gets so bad the dollar is worthless in a few weeks?

What if the cost of living becomes more expensive, so expensive, in fact, that it takes more money to live on than I had expected?

What if I go wild and spend too much on books and designer clothes and trips out of town?

Once you have listed absolutely everything you can think of that could possibly go wrong with your life in Paris, look at each concern as clear-eyed as you can, and ask your-self the following questions:

How likely is it that these things will happen?

Even if you are wearing a really drab practical hat, you really can't in good conscience believe that some of the wildly awful things that you have dreamed up have a snow-ball's chance in hell of actually occurring. Falling of the Eiffel Tower? Being kidnapped and shuttled off to work the mines? By really examining the possibility of any danger, we can begin to weed out the irrational fears. When you realize how silly some of them are, you can dismiss them as simply a distracting Noise. And remember your encour-ager friends? Be sure to ask them what they think about your concern about rats in the dungeon. See what they have to say about that, if you want to feel really silly!

Once you realize that your irrational fears are just Noise that had the potential of drowning out your dreams, push them over to the right-hand column, the Noise column, and forget them. Move on to the more realistic fears and look at them seriously and honestly. Your practical hat will require you to do some research in order to come up with realistic possibilities.

What if the exchange rate gets so bad the dollar is worthless in a few weeks?

Well, that is a possibility, although very remote. More likely would be that the exchange rate worsens significantly. In the last year, the worst it has been was about 1% lower than it is now. Lately it's been getting better. Realistically, I should consider that it could drop a percentage point or two and plan for that.

What if the cost of living becomes more expensive, so expensive, in fact, that it takes more money to live on than I had expected?

That is a valid point. If inflation becomes an issue, it could cost more than I anticipated, but there are no signs of excessive inflation at this time. Realistically, it probably wouldn't go up more than a percentage point or two.

What if I go wild and spend too much on books and designer clothes and trips out of town?

Frankly, that will be tempting. Can I control that?

Creative Thinking

All done? Sure you can't think of anything else that might be a problem? If not, take off your critical thinking hat and put your fun hat back on. Time to get creative again, and begin countering each of the possible dangers. Ask yourself:

What can I do to prevent these things from happening?

And then, writing as fast and furiously as you can, come up with possible solutions:

Deteriorating exchange rate: How about I go ahead and exchange my dollars to Euros now so that fluctuations in currency won't affect my purchasing power? That takes care of the weakening dollar fear.

Inflationary pressures: I should pick out the area I want to live and start looking for an apartment. If I sign a lease and lock in the price before I leave, that would take care of the possible increase in rent. I should calculate the current cost of food and include eating out at least once a day. That way, I will have a clue of how much things might go up if inflation heats up by 1, 2 or 3%. But if food costs do go up, I can eat out less frequently.

What if I go wild and spend too much? I really should make a budget and make sure I have a reasonable amount earmarked for shopping and sightseeing, and hopefully I will have enough will power not to get out of control. Maybe I should get an extra part-time job in the few months before I leave so I can set aside just a little more in case I run into a designer I just can't live without. As for sightseeing trips, maybe I can find a companion to share the cost of a car and lodging so we can conserve. I'll post an ad as soon as I get there to find one.

You can spend a lot of time being creative here. Keep working at it until you are satisfied that such a fate is not likely to happen. You can generate many ideas that will lead to other ideas that will lead to. . . who knows what? At this point, you may begin to see that Paris is really possible for you. Your creative imaginings can boost your confidence and make you aware of how valuable your Life Worth Assets are. Keeping your creative hat on, move on to the next issue:

What could I do to mitigate the problem if it does happen?

Deteriorating exchange rate: Not an issue if I already have made the currency exchange before leaving.

Inflationary pressures: Most of the problem can be taken care of by changing my behavior. Eat out less, buy less. Maybe I can start a supper club. It would be a good way to get to know people, and we could be social without going out if we took turns cooking for each other. I could always cut my trip short. I might be able to get a job. The last time I was in Paris, I saw a sign in a shop window advertising for English-speaking help. Maybe I could talk a friend into joining me for a few months and sharing the rent. If necessary, I could move to a cheaper place.

Going wild and spending too much: Again, I can control my behavior, and cut back, or perhaps get a job or roommate if I have to.

As you can see, it doesn't take much imagination or effort to think through the very scary prospect of running out of money and finding ways to lay those fears to rest. But keep that creative hat on! Keep scribbling ideas. If you think about it long enough, not only can you find ways to keep from running out of money while you are in Paris, but maybe you can even find ways to make money while you are there.

How about you find a fabulous clothing designer who has not been introduced in the US yet and import her line into the American market? What if you set up a service paving the way for other Americans to come to Paris? You could find apartments and roommates; make arrangements for daytrips and overnight tours to sites outside Paris.

You could set up classes in conversational English and teach Parisians the fine art of putting their "r's" in the front of the mouth. You could set up cooking classes in American cuisine—Southern fried chicken and barbecued ribs. You could provide a service catering home cooked American meals to other American ex-pats around town. The opportunities are limited only by your Imagination and Creativity.

Practical Thinking/Creative Thinking

When you have absolutely run out of great ideas, put your practical hat back on again. It's time to examine those crazy ideas about how to keep from going broke while in Paris from the pessimistic perspective. Of course, you'll end up weeding out a lot of your more brilliant ideas, but give each one a fair shot by letting the optimist in you look at it again. Maybe an idea that is inherently a failure can be tweaked until it becomes a real jewel. It might lead you to a new idea that is slightly related, but different. Don't be afraid to explore the seeming hopeless. You can't unearth gems unless you dig through a lot of dirt.

By the way, when you are packing for the big move, be sure you leave room for both hats. You're going to need them while you're in Paris. But my guess is, your creative hat will get bigger and prettier while you are there. The nice thing about these hats is they get worn out only from neglect. The more you wear them and use them, the better they get. And the better they get, the better your Queendom gets.

TRUST YOURSELF

You have to trust yourself, be what you are, and do what you ought to do the way you should do it. You have got to discover you, what you do, and trust it.

~Barbara Streisand

I hope you have found this little adventure as enlightening and as life-changing as I have. As we have been exploring our Queendoms together, I have made some startling discoveries about myself, and I have been amazed at the changes I have made in my own life.

A lot has happened during the last three years as I have conceived, researched, and written this little labor of love. Alas, I have given up my Dream of hiking the Appalachian Trail, but have substituted a more manageable resolve of going to the mountains and hiking more frequently on the weekends. Last summer and fall, Mike and I began making several exploratory trips, and we discovered many new and wonderful places. We usually spend our time in the Tennessee and North Carolina mountains, but lately, we have begun to explore Virginia as well, and that has led me to realize how interesting Civil War history is. This is opening new avenues for me.

I also have begun to work out more regularly so that I can hike more extensively, and I have revived my old love for theatre and performance by joining a theatre group. I joined a church and a writing group, and I now limit my hours in front of the TV. I am taking better care of my health by changing my eating habits. I encouraged my daughter, Mary Elizabeth to expand her business as a full time artist. I put my house on the market in anticipation of drastically downsizing so Mike and I can travel more, and even consider living abroad for a while. I made some important changes in my own business. I started an official support group with some good friends to encourage each other's Dreams.

I hope you have made some interesting discoveries about yourself, and have made some dramatic changes as well. Although you may have had some painful moments as you examined your life, I hope you have come to respect and honor your own desires and Ambitions, and to celebrate the truly unique person that you are. By now, you should have recognized that you are extraordinarily wealthy. You have a whole storehouse of treasures that you never realized you had before. No one has exactly the same Ambitions and

Dreams that you do. No one has the Drive to achieve those specific Dreams like you do. No one has the same combination of Life Worth Assets that are specific to you.

Now, if you have taken the principals outlined in this book to heart, you have made and tempered and sharpened your Nails by learning to think creatively, productively, and systematically, and you have hammered your Horseshoes onto your Horses' hoofs. You have ousted the treacherous enemies of your Queendom and have knighted the Riders who are true to it. You also are prepared for any contingency as you keep your Thoughts, Actions, Strategies and Goals consistent with your deep values and you keep your eyes and heart on your Vision. Now it is time to put on your crown and issue your orders. All of your Riders and your Horses are ready to do your bidding.

Your Queendom shimmers before you. Yiiiii-Ha! Into the breach, dear friends!

Wherever you go, go with all your heart.
~Confucius

ENDNOTES

Foreword:
1. Mark Kurlansky, *Salt: A World History* (New York: Penguin Books, 2003), p. 63
2. Jack Weatherford, *The History of Money* (New York: Three Rivers Press, 1997) p. 61-62.
3. IBID, p. 22.
4. IBID, p. 17.
5. IBID, p. 23.
6. IBID, p. 126.

Chapter 1: The Herstory of Money
1. Brian Hayden, "Pathways to Power: Principles for Creating Socioeconomic Inequalities," in T. Douglas Price and Gary Feinman, *Images of the Past* (New York: Plenum Press, 1995), p. 21.
2. Jack Weatherford, *The History of Money* (New York: Three Rivers Press, 1997), p. 30.
3. E.J. Graff, *What is Marriage For?* (Boston: Beacon Press, 2004), p. 5-7.
4. Antonia Fraser, *The Weaker Vessel* (New York: Alfred A. Knopf, 1984), p. 10.
5. Stephanie Coontz, *Marriage, a History: How Love Conquered Marriage* (New York: Penguin Group, 2005), p. 115.
6. Jack Weatherford, *The History of Money* (New York: Three Rivers Press, 1997), p. 32.
7. IBID, p. 40.
8. IBID, p. 41.
9. IBID, p. 48.
10. IBID, p. 61.

11. Stephanie Coontz, *Marriage, a History: How Love Conquered Marriage* (New York: Penguin Group, 2005), p. 113-115.

12. IBID, p. 91-92.

13. IBID, p. 103.

14. IBID.

15. Antonia Fraser, *The Weaker Vessel* (New York: Alfred A. Knopf, 1984), p. 10.

16. Stephanie Coontz, *Marriage, a History: How Love Conquered Marriage* (New York: Penguin Group, 2005), p. 16-18.

17. E.J. Graff, *What is Marriage For?* (Boston: Beacon Press, 2004), p. 5.

18. Stephanie Coontz, *Marriage, a History: How Love Conquered Marriage* (New York: Penguin Group, 2005), p. 16.

19. Antonia Fraser, *The Weaker Vessel* (New York: Alfred A. Knopf, 1984), p. 97-98.

20. IBID, p. 100.

21. E.J. Graff, *What is Marriage For?* (Boston: Beacon Press, 2004), p. 10-12.

22. Stephanie Coontz, *Marriage, a History: How Love Conquered Marriage* (New York: Penguin Group, 2005), p. 156.

23. IBID, p. 155-156.

24. IBID, p. 7.

25. IBID, p. 146.

26. E.J. Graff, *What is Marriage For?* (Boston: Beacon Press, 2004), p. 30.

27. See in *Playboy*: Bob Norman, "Miss Gold Digger of 1953" (undated first issue).

28. Niall Ferguson, *The Ascent of Money* (New York: The Penguin Press, 2008), p. 279.

29. Stephanie Coontz, *Marriage, a History: How Love*

Conquered Marriage (New York: Penguin Group, 2005), p. 268.

30. Niall Ferguson, *The Ascent of Money* (New York: The Penguin Press, 2008), p. 279.

31. Hannah Hoag, "Sex on the Brain," *New Scientist*, July 19, 2008.

32. Paula Ebben, "Research Suggests Women Better Investors Than Men," *CBS News Boston*, Nov 16, 2010.

33. Niall Ferguson, *The Ascent of Money* (New York: The Penguin Press, 2008), p. 280.

34. Jack Weatherford, *The History of Money* (New York: Three Rivers Press, 1997), p. 3.

35. For more discussion on oxytocin's effects, see: Deborah Blum, *Sex on the Brain* (New York: Penguin Group, 1997); and Louann Brizendine, *The Female Brain* (New York: Broadway Books, 2006).

Chapter 2: Living Well in a Place of Plenty

1. Daniel Akst, "A Talk with Betsey Stevenson and Justin Wolfers," *Boston Globe*, November 23, 2008.

2. IBID

3. James K. Wilson, N.D., D.C., PhD., *Adrenal Fatigue: The 21ˢᵗ Century Stress Syndrome*

4. Per Björntorp, "Body Fat Distribution, Insulin Resistance, and Metabolic Diseases," *Nutrition*, 13, July 1997, 795-803; also Per Björntorp, "Do Stress Reactions Cause Abdominal Obesity and Comorbidities?" *Obesity Reviews*, 2, February 2001, 73-86. Also Wilson, p 7.

5. Brian Rose, *Life Redefined* (Xulon Press, 2009), p. 71.

6. Sharon Jayson, "Happiness: Staying Positive in Negative Territory," USA Today, August 6, 2009.

7. Marilyn Elias, "Psychologists Now Know What Makes People Happy," USA Today, December 8, 2002.

8. Jerome Kagan, *Galen's Prophesy: Temperament in*

Human Nature (Boulder, Colorado: Westview Press, 1998).

9. Kristen A. Moore, James L. Peterson, and Frank Furstenberg, "Parental Attitudes and the Occurrence of Early Sexual Activity," *Journal of Marriage and Family*, 48, November 1986, 777-782.

10. Leaf Van Boven and Thomas Gilovich, "To Do or To Have: That Is the Question," *Journal of Personality and Social Psychology*, 85, December 2003, 1195-1202; and Elizabeth Landau, "Study: Experiences Make Us Happier Than Possessions," *CNN.com*, February 10, 2009 http://www.cnn.com/2009/HEALTH/02/10/happiness.poss essions/index.html

11. Mihaly Csikszentmihalyi, *Finding Flow: The Psychology of Engagement with Everyday Life* (New York: Basic Books, 1997), p. 29-32.

12. According to USA Today, 8/6/2009, recent studies have shown that high levels of gratitude increases happiness in humans.

13. Cecile Andrews, *Slow is Beautiful: New Visions of Community, Leisure and Joie de Vivre* (Canada: New Society Publishers, 2006), p. 19.

Chapter 3: The Role of Money

1. Alan Duke, "Nicolas Cage Caused His Own Financial Ills, Ex-Business Manager Says," *CNN.com*, November 18, 2009 http://www.cnn.com/2009/ SHOWBIZ/11/17/ icolas.cage.lawsuit/index.html

Chapter 4: Net Worth vs. Life Worth

1. Louann Brizendine, The Female Brain (New York: Broadway Books, 2006), p. 14.
2. Deborah Blum, *Sex on the Brain* (New York: Penguin Group, 1997), p. 46-48.
3. Louann Brizendine, *The Female Brain* (New York: Broadway Books, 2006), p. 14.
4. Martin Hoffman, "Sex Differences in Empathy and Related Behaviors," *Psychological Bulletin*, 84, July 1977, 712-722; and Abraham Sagi and Martin Hoffman, "Empathic Distress in the Newborn," *Developmental Psychology*, 12, March 1976, 175-176.
5. Sally and Bennett Shaywitz, et al, "Sex Differences in the Functional Organization of the Brain for Language," *Nature, 373, February 1995, 607-609.*
6. Naomi Rotter, "Sex Differences in Encoding and Decoding of Negative Facial Emotions," *Journal of Nonverbal Behavior, 12,* June 1988, 139-148.
7. Sandra Witelsen, "Women Have Greater Density of Neurons in Posterior Temporal Cortex*" Journal of Neuroscience*, 15, May 1995, 3418-3428.
8. Bruce Naliboff and Steven Berman, et al, "Sex-Related Differences in IBS Patients: Central Processing of Visceral Stimuli," *Gastroenterology*, 124, June 2003, 1738-47.
9. Louann Brizendine, *The Female Brain* (New York: Broadway Books, 2006), p. 14, 21.
10. IBID, p. 37-38.
11. Bruce Naliboff and Steven Berman, et al, "Sex-Related Differences in IBS Patients: Central Processing of Visceral Stimuli," *Gastroenterology*, 124, June 2003, 1738-47.

12. Harvey Mackay, *Fired Up: How the Best of the Best Survived and Thrived After Getting the Boot* (New York: Ballantine Books, 2005), p. 240.

13. "Merrill Lynch Investment Managers (MLIM) Survey Finds: When It Comes to Investing, Gender a Strong Influence on Behavior," April 18, 2005 http://www.ml.com/index.asp?id=7695_7696_8149_46028_47486_47543#contacts

14. Alexander Conrad, "Finance Basics Elude Citizens," *Harvard-Crimson*, February 2, 2008.

15. Princeton Survey Research Associates International, "Financial Literacy Survey," prepared for the National Foundation for Credit Counseling, April 19, 2007.

16. Niall Ferguson, *The Ascent of Money* (New York: The Penguin Press, 2008), p. 13-14.

Chapter 7: Making it Happen

1. Rob Walters, *Spread Spectrum: Hedy Lamarr and the Mobile Phone* (BookSurge Publishing, 2006).

Chapter 9: Nails

1. Michael Michalko, *Thinkertoys* (Berkeley: Ten Speed Press, 2006), p. 378.

2. Louann Brizendine, *The Female Brain* (New York: Broadway Books, 2006), p. 91.

3. IBID, p. 23.

4. IBID, p. 5 and p. 91.

5. Deborah Blum, *Sex on the Brain* (New York: Penguin Group, 1997), p. 47-48 and p. 61.

6. Louann Brizendine, *The Female Brain* (New York: Broadway Books, 2006), p. 40-41; and Joseph Carver, "Emotional Memory Management: Positive Control Over Your Memory," 2005 http://www.drjoecarver.com/clients/49355/File/Emotional%20Memory.html

7. Julie Norem, *The Positive Power of Negative Thinking* (Cambridge, MA: Basic Books, 2001).

8. Norman Doidge, *The Brain That Changes Itself* (New York: Penguin Books, 2007).

9. Tom Morris, *True Success: A New Philosophy of* Excellence (Berkeley: Berkeley Books, 1994), p. 38

10. IBID, p. 43.

11. Tim Hurson, *Think Better: An Innovator "s Guide to Productive Thinking* (New York: McGraw-Hill Books, 2008), p. 64.

BIBLIOGRAPHY

Andrews, Cecile. *Slow is Beautiful: New Visions of Community, Leisure and Joie de Vivre.* Canada: New Society Publishers, 2006.

Akst, Daniel. "A Talk with Betsy Stevenson and Justin Wolfers." *Boston Globe,* November 23, 2008.

Björntorp, Per. "Body Fat Distribution, Insulin Resistance, and Metabolic Diseases." *Nutrition* 13 (July 1997).

Björntorp, Per. "Do Stress Reactions Cause Abdominal Obesity and Comorbidities." *Obesity Reviews* 2 (February 2001).

Blum, Deborah. *Sex on the Brain: The Biological Differences between Men and Women.* New York: Penguin Books, 1998.

Bodnar, Janet. *Money Smart Women: Everything You Need to Know to Achieve a Lifetime of Financial Security.* Chicago: Kaplan Publishing, 2006.

Brizendine, Louann. *The Female Brain.* New York: Broadway Books, 2006.

Carver, Joseph. "Emotional Memory Management: Positive Control Over Your Memory." 2005. http://www.drjoecarver.com/clients/49355/File/Emotional%20Memory.html

Condren, Debra. *Ambition Is Not a Dirty Word: A Woman's Guide to Earning Her Worth and Achieving Her Dreams.* New York: Broadway Books, 2006.

Conrad, Alexander. "Finance Basics Elude Citizens." *Harvard-Crimson, February 2, 2008.*

Coontz, Stephanie. *Marriage, a History: How Love Conquered Marriage.* New York: Penguin Books, 2006.

Csikszentmihalyi, Mihaly. *Finding Flow: The Psychology of Engagement with Everyday Life.* New York: Basic Books, 1997.

Doidge, Norman. *The Brain That Changes Itself: Stories of Personal Triumph from the Frontiers of Brain Science.* New York: Penguin Books, 2007.

Duke, Alan. "Nicolas Cage Caused His Own Financial-Ills, Ex-Business Manager Says." *CNN.com*, November 18, 2009.

Ebben, Paula. "Research Suggests Women Better Investors Than Men." *CBS News Boston.* November 16, 2010

Elias, Marilyn. "Psychologists Now Know What Makes People Happy." *USA Today*, December 8, 2002.

Evans, Heidi. *How to Hide Money From Your Husband: The Best Kept Secret of Marriage.* New York: Simon & Schuster, 1999.

Ferguson, Niall. *The Ascent of Money: A Financial History of the World.* New York: Penguin Press, 2008.

Fraser, Antonia. *The Weaker Vessel.* New York: Knopf, 1984.

Graff, E.J. *What is Marriage For?: A Strange Social History of Our Most Intimate Institution.* Boston: Beacon Press, 2004.

Hayden, Brian. "Pathways to Power: Principles for Creating Socioeconomic Inequalities." *Images of the*

Past, by T. Douglas Price and Gary Feinman. New York: Plenum Press, 1995.

Hoag, Hannah. "Sex on the brain." *New Scientist*. July 19, 2008.

Hoffman, Martin. "Sex Differences in Empathy and Related Behaviors." *Psychological Bulletin* 84 (July 1977).

Hoffman, Martin, and Abraham Sagi. "Empathic Distress in the Newborn." *Developmental Psychology* 12 (March 1976).

Hurson, Tim. *Think Better: An Innovator's Guide to Productive Thinking*. New York: McGraw-Hill Books, 2008.

Jayson, Sharon. "Happiness: Staying Positive in Negative Territory." *USA Today,* August 6, 2009.

Kagan, Jerome. Galen's Prophesy: Temperament in Human Nature. Boulder, Colorado: Westview Press, 1998.

Kurlansky, Mark. *Salt: A World History*. New York: Penguin Books, 2003.

Landau, Elizabeth. "Study: Experiences Make Us Happier Than Possessions." *CNN.com*, February 10, 2009.

Mackay, Harvey. *Fired Up: How the Best of the Best Survived and Thrived After Getting the Boot*. New York: Ballantine Books, 2005.

"Merrill Lynch Investment Managers (MLIM) Survey Finds: When It Comes to Investing, Gender A Strong Influence on Behavior," April 18, 2005.

Michalko, Michael. *Cracking Creativity: The Secrets of Creative Genius.* Berkeley, Calif.: Ten Speed Press, 2001.

Michalko, Michael. *Thinkertoys.* Berkeley, Calif.: Ten Speed Press, 2006.

Moore, Kristen A., James L. Peterson, and Frank Furstenberg, "Parental Attitudes and the Occurrence of Early Sexual Activity." *Journal of Marriage and Family* 48 (November 1986).

Morris, Tom. *True Success: A New Philosophy of Excellence.* New York: Berkley Books, 1995.

Naliboff, Bruce, and Steve Berman, et al. "Sex-Related Differences in IBS Patients: Central Processing of Visceral Stimuli." *Gastroenterology* 124 (June 2003).

Norem, Julie. *The Positive Power of Negative Thinking.* Cambridge, MA: Basic Books, 2001.

Pegues, Deborah Smith. *30 Days to Taming Your Finances: What to Do (and Not Do) to Better Manage Your Money.* Eugene, Oregon: Harvest House Publishers, 2006.

Princeton Survey Research Associates International. "Financial Literacy Survey," prepared for the National Foundation for Credit Counseling, April 19, 2007.

Rose, Brian. *Life Re.Defined.* Xulon Press, 2009.

Rotter, Naomi. "Sex Differences in Encoding and Decoding of Negative Facial Emotions." *Journal of Nonverbal Behavior* 12 (June 1988).

Sass, Erik and Steve Wiegand. *The Mental Floss History of the World: An Irreverent Romp Through Civilization's Best Bits*. New York: HarperCollins, 2008.

Shaywitz, Sally, and Bennett Shaywitz, et al. "Sex Differences in the Functional Organization of the Brain for Language." *Nature* 373 (February 1995).

Taylor-Hough, Deborah. *Frugal Living for Dummies: Practical Ideas to Help You Spend Less, Save More, and Live Well*. New York: Wiley Publishing, 2003.

Van Boven, Leaf, and Thomas Gilovich. "To Do or to Have: That Is the Question." *Journal of Personality and Social Psychology* 85 (December 2003).

Walters, Rob. *Spread Spectrum: Hedy Lamarr and the Mobile Phone*. BookSurge Publishing, 2006.

Weatherford, Jack. *The History of Money*. New York: Three Rivers Press, 1997.

Wilson, James L. Adrenal Fatigue: The 21st Century Stress Syndrome. Petaluma, CA: Smart Publications, 2001.

Witelsen, Sandra. "Women Have Greater Density of Neurons in Posterior Temporal Cortex." *Journal of Neuroscience* 15 (May 1995).

Deborah Griffitts Hining

INDEX

Pamplona: 137, 144-7, 149
Parks, Rosa: 112, 147
Parton, Dolly: 102
Pessimists: 190-3
Playboy Magazine: 27
Pope Gregory VII: 18
Positive-thinking: 91
Poverty: 6, 16, 31, 33, 37, 102
Power: 10-3, 16-20, 23, 24, 34, 60, 67, 103, 116, 186, 187, 203, 204
Practical Sex: 31
Premenstrual tension: 41
Presley, Elvis: 65
Princeton University: 95
Procreation: 21
Prostitution: 12
Puberty: 80, 81
Purchasing power: 203
Recipe for the good life: 53
Remick, Lee: 48
Respiratory infections: 41
Retail Therapy: 50, 51
Richard III: 144
Right brain hemisphere(s): 187
Roman Empire: 4, 15
Rowling, J K: 102
Sandburg, Carl: 109
Sasson, Remez: 182, 196
Schopenhauer, Arthur: 129
Schultz, Charles: 107
Self-actualization: 38
Self-esteem: 52
Serotonin: 188
Sexual drive: 186
Shakespeare: 20, 125, 144, 195
Social connection: 187
Social currencies: 9
Socrates: 59
Soul Food(s): 123-127, 130, 155
Spencer, Diana: 88
Spirituality: 59, 100, 124, 130
Stanley, Bessie Anderson: 37
Stevenson, Betsey: 39
Stewart, James: 48
Streisand, Barbara: 206
Stress: 41, 47

Synapse(s): 179, 180, 194
Talmud: 120
Tangible commodities: 11
Tangible resource: 34
Tax: 29, 75, 95, 105, 158
Testosterone: 79, 80
Thoreau: 139
Tufano, Peter: 95
Ugly pessimists: 194
Van Boven, Leaf: 54
Van Pelt, Lucy: 107
Victoria: 131
Voltaire, François-Marie: 14
Weatherford, Jack: 65
Whatifs: 90-2
Whole brain: 186
Widows' rights: 21
Wilson, James: 41
Winfrey, Oprah: 102
Wolfers, Justin: 39
Woods, Tiger: 49
Xenophon: 14
Yesbuts: 92
You're a Good Man Charlie Brown: 107

Deborah Griffitts Hining

About the Author

Deborah Griffitts Hining, is a financial advisor located in Chapel Hill, NC who believes that financial planning begins with a close and honest examination of one's most heartfelt desires. Once people know what they really want from life, they can focus all the assets available to them to make their dreams come to fruition. She has been practicing financial planning since 1993 and is a Certified Financial Planner™, Chartered Retirement Planning Counselor, Chartered Life Underwriter, and Chartered Financial Consultant. She also holds a PhD Degree from Louisiana State University.

Of late, her interests have led her to research the impact of gender differences in investment styles and planning needs. It has become her vocation to help women understand and use their innate strengths and abilities—dreams and desires, intelligence and skills, ambition and tenacity, among many others—to help them build the lives they most earnestly yearn for. She believes that women must be encouraged to believe in themselves and what they are capable of attaining. *Money is No Object* is the first practical guide to help women discover and honor their resources, build upon them, and use them to create a life well lived.

The author lives in North Carolina, with her husband Michael and enjoys traveling, gardening, lecturing, and rescuing derelict old houses. She can be reached at dhining@gmail.com.

More from Deborah Hining

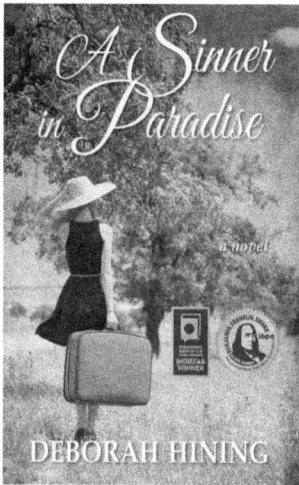

A Sinner in Paradise

A heartwarming, uproarious affair with love in all its forms. Jilted by her fiance, Geneva returns to her native hills of West Virginia where she plans to rest and heal from her heartbreak. When Geneva's ambition, and machinations run up against rugged mountain ways, she finds herself flung from one perilous adventure, romance, crazy circumstance, and heartbreak to another.

A Saint in Graceland

Grieving her mother's death and yearning to see more of the world beyond her mountain home, Sally Beth sets out on a journey that leads her across the American Southwest and ultimately to a remote mission station in Tanzania, where she finds a new kind of freedom in the African plains and the people who dwell there. But when war comes to the mission gates, its horrors shakes her world. She must find a way to rebuild her life and choose whether or not to serve the people she's grown to love—a choice that will shake the simple faith of her childhood and ignite her passion for a wounded man.

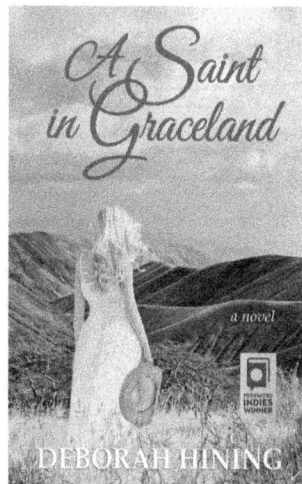

In the Midst of Innocence

An endearing ballad of the struggle for existence and understanding. Ten-year-old Pearl Wallace is living in the mountains of rural Tennessee in the depths of the Great Depression. Pearl struggles with her moral dilemma: How much does she need to tithe on the money she has earned from stealing her daddy's moonshine and selling it? Meanwhile, Emily Weston, a missionary, has come to "lift the poor hillbillies of the region out of their ignorance and misery." Coming from a place of affluence and privilege, she is quickly overwhelmed by the social and racial issues facing her students and their families.

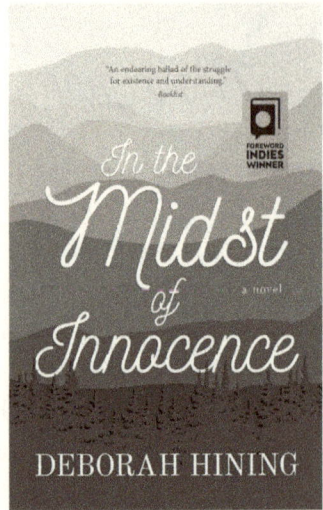

www.ingramcontent.com/pod-product-compliance
Lightning Source LLC
Chambersburg PA
CBHW020154200326
41521CB00006B/356